BUILD A WORDPRESS WEBSITE

FROM SCRATCH

WordPress 6.4

2024

RAPHAEL HEIDE

Build a WordPress Website From Scratch 2024

Published by raphaelheide.com

Heide, Raphael: Build a WordPress Website From Scratch 2024

We are thrilled to announce the release of the latest edition of "Build a WordPress Website From Scratch 2024" This comprehensive guide empowers you to create stunning and professional websites using WordPress. With the inclusion of the 6.4 WordPress update for 2024, you'll have access to the most up-to-date information and techniques.

"Build a WordPress Website From Scratch 2024" caters to both beginners and seasoned users, offering a step-by-step approach to constructing your ideal website. Whether you're launching a business site, an affiliate platform, a personal hobby site, or a blog, this book serves as your trusted companion throughout the entire website-building process.

Should you have any questions, I encourage you to contact me via email at contact@raphaelheide.com.

Thank you to my readers

I deeply appreciate your choice to embark on this WordPress website-building journey with our book. In a sea of available resources, your decision to entrust us with your learning experience is a tremendous honor. My ultimate aim has always been to provide you with a comprehensive and current guide that equips you to craft extraordinary websites confidently and effortlessly.

I sincerely hope that the knowledge and techniques shared within these pages have proven invaluable in your pursuit of constructing the website of your dreams. The process of website creation can often seem daunting, but my aspiration has been to demystify it, ensuring accessibility for beginners and experienced users alike. Your unwavering commitment to learning and growth is nothing short of commendable, and it fills me with immense pride to be a part of your educational journey.

I must also take this moment to extend our heartfelt gratitude to those of you who have reached out with questions, feedback, and suggestions. Your engagement and interaction are the lifeblood of our endeavor. Continuously, I strive to enhance and refine our content, and your valuable input plays a pivotal role in delivering an improved experience to our readers.

In closing, I wish to extend an open invitation for you to maintain a connection with me. Whether you seek further guidance, have lingering questions, or simply wish to share your success stories, please do not hesitate to reach out. Your ongoing support is a source of great motivation, and I remain steadfast in my commitment to assisting you in all your WordPress website endeavors.

Once more, thank you for being an integral part of our readership. Your unwavering enthusiasm and dedication inspire us to continue creating valuable content, empowering individuals like yourself to realize their website-building aspirations. May your path be paved with continued success and fulfillment in all your future endeavors.

Warm regards,

Raphael Heide

Welcome

Welcome to the dynamic and diverse world of WordPress, and congratulations on choosing this book as your guide! Within these pages, you'll discover a comprehensive resource designed to help you navigate the boundless possibilities of WordPress and empower you to create truly remarkable websites.

As you delve into the rich content of this book, it's essential to keep in mind that the terminology and concepts discussed may vary slightly depending on your country or region. While we strive to provide universal guidance, the vibrant WordPress community often adapts and evolves, so it's always a good practice to verify and customize specific terms and practices based on your local resources and WordPress community.

Rest assured, this book is meticulously tailored to the latest version of WordPress, ensuring that you're armed with the most pertinent and up-to-date information. Whether you're using the current version of WordPress or have recently updated your installation, you can confidently follow along, applying the provided instructions and techniques.

To maximize your experience with this book, we recommend having a basic understanding of computers and feeling comfortable with fundamental web browsing. No prior experience with WordPress is required, as this book will expertly guide you through each step, commencing with the fundamentals and gradually advancing to more intricate topics.

Within the chapters, you'll encounter crystal-clear explanations, pragmatic examples, and interactive exercises designed to reinforce your understanding. Take your time to absorb the wealth of information provided, and don't hesitate to revisit any sections that may require further clarification. Remember, the journey of learning WordPress is a marathon, not a sprint, and this book stands as your steadfast companion throughout this enriching expedition.

So, grab your preferred beverage, locate a cozy corner, and prepare to embark on this exhilarating adventure of mastering WordPress. Prepare to unlock your creative potential, construct impressive websites, and tap into the vast realm of possibilities within the WordPress ecosystem. Together, let's dive into the depths of knowledge and make the most of this extraordinary resource!

Always bear in mind that the landscape of website building is ever-evolving, and technology continuously advances. Stay curious, embrace change, and enjoy the exciting challenge of harnessing the power of WordPress. Happy reading and happy building!

For Your Information

We hope you enjoyed reading this book and learned something new from it. As a bonus, I have prepared some additional resources for you to explore further. At the end of this book, you will find supporting materials, such as links to high-resolution images and much more. These materials will help you deepen your understanding of the topics covered in this book and apply them to your own projects. You can also share them with your friends and colleagues who might be interested in this book. Thank you for choosing this book and we hope to hear from you soon.

Table of Contents

The difference of this book is that it does not require any prior knowledge in web programming. WordPress offers simplified methods to create complete websites with management done through a control panel. The book explains step by step how to use these features and how to customize the site according to the preferences of the reader.

(1) WordPress - A Comprehensive Introduction

In the vast realm of website creation, one name stands out as a beacon of innovation and versatility—WordPress. But what exactly is WordPress? To put it simply, WordPress is a content management system (CMS) that allows users to build and manage websites with ease.

At its core, WordPress is an open-source platform, meaning that its source code is freely available for anyone to use, modify, and enhance. This accessibility has fueled its rapid growth and

widespread adoption, making it the go-to choice for both beginners and seasoned developers alike.

With WordPress, the possibilities are endless. Whether you aspire to create a personal blog, an e-commerce store, a corporate website, or even a thriving online community, WordPress provides a solid foundation upon which to build your digital empire.

User-Friendly Interface and Themes

One of the key features that sets WordPress apart is its user-friendly interface. Even those with limited technical expertise can navigate its intuitive dashboard, allowing for seamless website management. From adding new pages and blog posts to customizing themes and installing plugins, WordPress empowers users to take control of their online presence.

Speaking of themes, WordPress offers a vast library of pre-designed templates that dictate the overall look and feel of your website. These themes provide a quick and convenient way to give your site a professional appearance without the need for extensive coding knowledge. With just a few clicks, you can transform the visual aesthetics of your website, aligning it with your unique brand identity.

Powerful Plugin Ecosystem

But the true power of WordPress lies in its extensive plugin ecosystem. Plugins are additional software components that can be seamlessly integrated into your WordPress website, enhancing its functionality and extending its capabilities. Whether you need to optimize your site for search engines, incorporate social media sharing buttons, or add advanced security measures, there is a plugin available to meet your needs.

Another noteworthy aspect of WordPress is its commitment to search engine optimization (SEO). With built-in features and plugins specifically designed to boost your website's visibility in search engine rankings, WordPress empowers you to optimize your content and attract organic traffic.

Furthermore, WordPress fosters a vibrant community of developers, designers, and enthusiasts who actively contribute to its growth and evolution. This thriving ecosystem ensures that WordPress remains at the forefront of web development trends and continually introduces new features and improvements.

The Rich History of WordPress

WordPress, as we know it today, has an intriguing history that dates back to the early 2000s. It emerged from humble beginnings, gradually evolving into the world's most popular content management system (CMS). To understand its journey, we must delve into the story of its creator, the development milestones, and the community that shaped its growth.

The origins of WordPress can be traced back to a personal blogging software called b2/cafelog. It was developed by French programmer Michel Valdrighi in 2001. WordPress's co-founder, Matt Mullenweg, discovered b2/cafelog and recognized its potential. Inspired by its simplicity and the concept of open-source software, Matt collaborated with another developer, Mike Little, to create a fork of b2/cafelog. Thus, on May 27, 2003, WordPress was born.

The early versions of WordPress focused primarily on blogging functionality, offering users an accessible platform to share their thoughts and ideas online. As the user base grew, so did the demand for additional features and customization options. This led to the introduction of themes and plugins, allowing users to modify the appearance and extend the functionality of their WordPress sites.

WordPress gained significant traction in 2005 with the release of version 1.5, codenamed "Strayhorn." This version introduced themes as a core feature, enabling users to switch between different visual styles effortlessly. It marked a turning point in WordPress's evolution, transforming it into a versatile platform that could be adapted for various purposes beyond just blogging.

Over the years, WordPress continued to evolve and improve. Version 2.0, named "Duke," arrived in 2005, bringing significant enhancements, including a revamped administration interface and an improved plugin architecture. These updates solidified WordPress's reputation as a user-friendly CMS that catered to both beginners and advanced users.

The introduction of the WordPress Plugin Directory in 2008 revolutionized the ecosystem. Developers could now contribute their own plugins, making it easier for users to enhance their websites with additional functionality. The plugin repository quickly grew, offering a vast array of options ranging from SEO optimization to e-commerce integration.

In 2010, WordPress reached a major milestone with the release of version 3.0, dubbed "Thelonious." This version merged WordPress with the previously separate WordPress MU (Multi-User) project, allowing users to manage multiple sites from a single installation. It laid the foundation for WordPress's future as a powerful platform for website building.

As the popularity of WordPress skyrocketed, its global community flourished. WordCamps, community-organized conferences, began sprouting up around the world, fostering collaboration, knowledge sharing, and networking among WordPress enthusiasts. The community's dedication to the platform's growth played a crucial role in its success.

Modern Innovations and Global Dominance

In recent years, WordPress has embraced modern web development trends. With the introduction of the Gutenberg editor in WordPress 5.0 (2018), the content creation experience underwent a significant transformation. Gutenberg replaced the traditional editor with a block-based approach, allowing users to build rich, dynamic layouts using a visual interface.

The rise of mobile devices also influenced WordPress's development. With the increasing prevalence of smartphones and tablets, WordPress adapted by adopting responsive design principles. Websites built on WordPress became mobile-friendly, providing optimal user experiences across different screen sizes.

Today, WordPress powers over 40% of all websites on the internet. Its success can be attributed to its commitment to simplicity, extensibility, and the support of a passionate community. WordPress's open-source nature ensures that it remains a flexible and accessible platform, empowering individuals and businesses to create remarkable online experiences.

Looking Ahead to Version 6.0 and Beyond

WordPress is now up to version 6.0 and comes with new features and improvements. It continues to evolve, embracing emerging technologies and user demands. Its journey remains an ongoing saga as it cements its position as the go-to CMS, enabling people worldwide to build, manage, and share their digital visions with the world.

WordPress is a dynamic and versatile platform that empowers users to build and manage websites with ease. From its user-friendly interface to its extensive library of themes and plugins, WordPress provides a solid foundation for creating captivating online experiences. With WordPress, you have the power to shape your digital presence and unleash your creativity upon the world. So, let us delve deeper into the realm of WordPress, unraveling its intricacies and unlocking its full potential as we embark on our journey to build a WordPress website from scratch.

Wordpress Script Language

WordPress, a robust and adaptable content management system, offers support for an array of scripting languages that elevate its capabilities and customization potential. Within this segment, we'll delve into several scripting languages frequently employed alongside WordPress and delve into their importance in expanding and transforming the platform.

For Your Information

I'm excited to share with you that creating a WordPress website does not require any programming knowledge. Yes, you read that right! WordPress empowers individuals, businesses, and organizations to establish an online presence without the need for coding skills. This incredible feature is one of the reasons behind WordPress's immense popularity as a content management system (CMS).

So, how does WordPress make it possible for anyone, regardless of their technical background, to build and manage a website? It's all about the user-friendly interface and the way WordPress handles the complexities of script languages behind the scenes.

1. **PHP (Hypertext Preprocessor):** PHP is the primary scripting language used in WordPress. It is a server-side scripting language that powers the dynamic aspects of the platform. WordPress itself is written in PHP, making it essential for developers and users who want to customize or create themes, plugins, and functionality. PHP enables WordPress to interact with databases, handle user input, and generate dynamic content. Understanding PHP is crucial for developers looking to extend WordPress's core features or create custom solutions.

2. **JavaScript:** JavaScript is a client-side scripting language that enhances the interactivity and user experience of WordPress websites. It allows developers to add dynamic elements, perform actions based on user interactions, and manipulate content on the fly. JavaScript libraries like jQuery are commonly used in WordPress to simplify complex tasks, create sliders, implement AJAX functionality, and enhance the responsiveness of themes and plugins. JavaScript is also vital for integrating third-

party scripts, such as analytics or social media widgets, into WordPress sites.

3. **CSS (Cascading Style Sheets):** While not technically a scripting language, CSS plays a crucial role in WordPress by controlling the presentation and styling of websites. CSS is responsible for defining the layout, colors, fonts, and visual aspects of a WordPress theme. With CSS, developers can customize the appearance of WordPress sites, override default styles, and create unique designs. Understanding CSS is essential for WordPress users and developers who want to tailor the visual aesthetics of their websites and ensure a cohesive and professional look.

4. **HTML (Hypertext Markup Language):** HTML is the standard markup language used to structure the content of web pages. In WordPress, HTML is primarily generated dynamically by the PHP scripts and theme templates. However, WordPress users and developers may need to have a basic understanding of HTML to modify page structures, add custom elements, or optimize content for search engines. HTML tags are used to define headings, paragraphs, links, images, tables, and other elements that comprise the content of a WordPress site.

5. **SQL (Structured Query Language):** SQL is a language used for managing and querying databases, and it plays a vital role in WordPress. WordPress uses the MySQL database to store and retrieve data, including posts, pages, comments, user information, and settings. Although WordPress abstracts most database operations, understanding SQL can be beneficial for developers who need to optimize queries, create custom database tables, or perform advanced database operations within their themes or plugins.

6. **Shell Scripting:** Shell scripting, commonly using the Bash (Bourne Again Shell) language, can be employed to automate tasks and perform system-level operations related to WordPress. With shell scripting, developers can create scripts to automate WordPress installations, backups, updates, and maintenance tasks. Shell scripting is especially useful for managing WordPress installations on servers, streamlining administrative tasks, and performing routine operations efficiently.

7. **Other Scripting Languages:** WordPress also provides support for other scripting languages, either natively or through plugins. Some plugins allow the usage of languages like Python, Ruby, or Perl to extend WordPress functionality. These languages can be utilized for specific tasks or when developers are more comfortable working with them. However, it's important to note that PHP remains the dominant scripting language within the WordPress ecosystem, and extensive support and resources are available primarily for PHP-based development.

(2)
Register Your Own Domain

In the digital landscape of today, having a domain name is an absolute necessity for establishing a meaningful online presence. A domain name acts as the distinct address of your website, simplifying the process for visitors to locate and access your content. Whether you're crafting a personal blog, launching an e-commerce emporium, or establishing a business website, owning a domain name confers numerous advantages.

To begin, a domain name bestows a professional and trustworthy veneer to your online identity. Instead of relying on free subdomains or unwieldy URLs, a custom domain name imbues your website with a professional allure, bolstering your brand recognition. This not only fosters trust among your audience but also imparts an aura of authenticity and legitimacy.

Next, let's dive into the subject of domain name costs. The price of a domain name can fluctuate based on various factors, including the top-level domain (TLD) you opt for (.com, .org, .net, etc.), your choice of domain registrar, and any supplementary services or features you might select. On average, a domain name generally falls within the $10 to $20 per year range. However, premium or highly sought-after domain names can command a higher price tag.

It's worth noting that domain name pricing may vary between countries and registrars. Certain TLDs may be more expensive than others, particularly if they are in high demand. Additionally, some domain registrars may offer promotional discounts or package deals, making it prudent to explore different options to secure the most favorable price for your desired domain name.

When deciding on a domain name, deliberate over a moniker that mirrors your brand, is easy to recall, and aligns harmoniously with your website's purpose. Conscientious research is essential to confirm the availability of your desired domain name and to ensure that it isn't already trademarked by another entity.

Why is it Important to Have Your Own Domain?

Branding and Credibility: Your domain name plays a pivotal role in shaping your brand identity and establishing credibility. It serves as a distinctive and memorable online moniker that visitors can readily connect with your business or personal ventures. A domain that mirrors your brand exudes professionalism and trustworthiness.

Customization and Control: Ownership of your domain grants you total control over your website and email infrastructure. You can tailor the domain name to align seamlessly with your brand, select your preferred extensions (e.g., .com, .org, .net), and craft personalized email addresses (e.g., info@yourdomain.com). This level of customization empowers you to shape your online presence precisely as you envision it.

Consistency and Longevity: A self-owned domain guarantees consistency in your digital presence. Unlike social media platforms or free website hosting services, which can alter their policies or disappear altogether, a domain offers a stable and enduring online address that you can depend on for the long haul.

Search Engine Visibility: A domain containing relevant keywords can bolster your visibility in search engine results. When users seek specific products, services, or information associated with your domain, a well-optimized website can enhance your search rankings, attracting organic traffic and expanding your online reach.

Professional Email Communication: With your own domain, you can establish professional email addresses that match your domain name, like yourname@yourdomain.com. This not only elevates the quality of your communication but also fortifies your brand image, instilling confidence in your clients and associates.

Where Can You Register Domains?

Domain registrars play a pivotal role in the digital landscape, as they are the gatekeepers of the internet's addressing system. These companies are officially authorized to sell domain names and offer a suite of services to facilitate your online journey. Among the most renowned domain registrars are GoDaddy, Namecheap, and Google Domains.

However, domain registration isn't limited to standalone registrars. Many web hosting providers also offer domain registration services as part of their hosting packages. This option can be especially convenient if you plan to host your website with the same provider. Leading hosting providers that bundle domain registration with their services include Bluehost, SiteGround, and DreamHost.

Moreover, it's essential to note that some countries have designated registrars for their top-level domain extensions. For example, if you're eyeing a .uk domain, you can register it through the UK's official registry, Nominet. Utilizing country-specific registrars is particularly advisable for localized businesses or organizations seeking to establish a strong regional presence.

Beyond these options, a plethora of resellers and marketplaces exists where you can register domains. These platforms often offer competitive pricing and additional services to sweeten the deal. Notable examples encompass Sedo, Flippa, and BuyDomains.

Furthermore, for those in search of premium or highly coveted domain names, domain auctions and expired domain marketplaces are worth exploring. These platforms, exemplified by GoDaddy Auctions and NameJet, provide opportunities to bid on or purchase domains that were previously registered but are now available for new ownership.

When selecting a domain registrar, several factors merit consideration:

Pricing: Compare the registration fees and renewal costs of different registrars to ensure they align with your budget.

Domain Extensions: Examine the registrar's available domain extensions and their associated pricing, as certain extensions may be more costly than others.

Domain Management Tools: Evaluate the domain management features offered by the registrar, including DNS management, domain forwarding, and privacy protection.

Customer Support: Seek out a registrar known for reliable customer support, as you may require assistance with domain configuration or troubleshooting.

Registering your own domain is an imperative step in establishing a professional online presence and retaining control over your brand and website. It unlocks opportunities for branding, customization, enhanced search engine visibility, and professional email communication. Whether you opt for dedicated registrars, hosting providers, country-specific authorities, resellers, or domain auctions, make a thoughtful choice that aligns with your needs, offering competitive pricing, robust domain management tools, and dependable customer support to make the most of your domain registration experience.

(3)
Sign Up for Web Hosting

In the previous chapter, we discussed the pivotal role that having your own domain plays in establishing a strong online presence. Now, it's time to dive deeper into another critical aspect of managing a website: web hosting. Web hosting is essentially the foundation upon which your website is built, and it has a profound impact on the performance, reliability, and functionality of your online presence. In this chapter, we will explore the importance of web hosting and provide you with a comprehensive guide on how to sign up for a web hosting service.

Understanding the Importance of Web Hosting

Web hosting is like the digital real estate where your website resides. It involves the storage of all your website's files, databases, and content, making them accessible to users across the internet. Here's why web hosting is so vital:

> **Website Performance:** The quality of your web hosting service significantly affects your website's speed and performance.

A fast-loading site is crucial for user experience and can positively impact your search engine rankings.

Storage and Bandwidth: Web hosting provides you with the necessary storage space to store your website files, databases, images, and other content. It also offers bandwidth, which refers to the amount of data transferred between your website and its visitors. Sufficient storage and bandwidth are crucial to accommodate your website's growth and handle increased traffic.

Reliability: A reliable web hosting provider ensures that your website is accessible to visitors 24/7 without downtime. This reliability is essential for maintaining your online credibility and retaining users.

Customization and Control: With web hosting, you have full control over your website's configuration, design, and functionality. You can install and customize content management systems like WordPress, Joomla, or Drupal, and integrate various plugins, themes, and extensions to enhance your website's features and appearance.

Scalability: As your website grows, you may need more resources. A good web hosting service allows for scalability, ensuring your site can handle increased traffic and data without hiccups.

Security: Web hosting providers often offer security features like firewalls, SSL certificates, and regular backups, helping to protect your website from cyber threats and data loss.

Email Hosting: Many web hosting providers offer email hosting services, allowing you to create professional email addresses using your domain name (e.g., yourname@

yourdomain.com). This provides a cohesive brand identity and facilitates effective communication with your audience.

Technical Support: Quality web hosts provide technical support to assist you in case of issues or questions. This support is invaluable, especially if you're not an expert in web development.

Web hosting is a service that allows individuals and organizations to make their websites accessible on the internet. It involves storing website files, data, and content on a server that is connected to the internet. When someone types in a website's domain name or clicks on a link, their browser sends a request to the web hosting server, which then delivers the website's files back to the user's browser, allowing them to view and interact with the website.

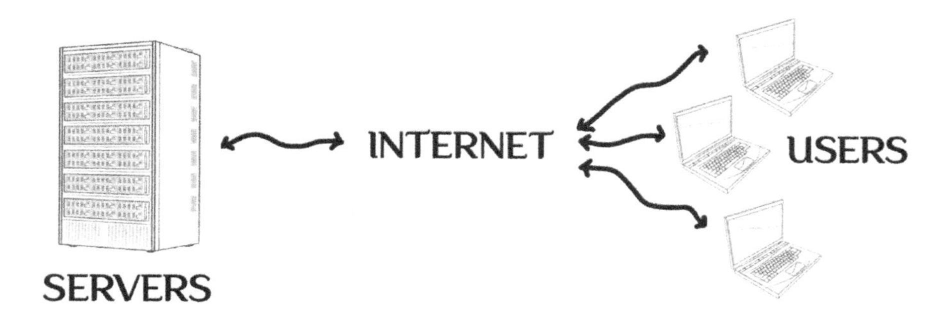

In simpler terms, web hosting provides the infrastructure and resources necessary to make a website available online 24/7. It ensures that the website is accessible to visitors from anywhere in the world, anytime they want to access it.

Examples of Web Hosting Providers

Bluehost: Bluehost is a widely recognized web hosting provider recommended by WordPress.org. It offers a range of hosting plans, including shared hosting, virtual private servers (VPS), and dedicated servers. Bluehost provides reliable performance, 24/7 customer support, and user-friendly control panels.

SiteGround: SiteGround is known for its excellent customer support and robust security features. They offer shared hosting, cloud hosting, and dedicated servers, with features like free SSL certificates, daily backups, and a user-friendly interface.

HostGator: is a popular choice for beginners due to its affordable shared hosting plans. They provide a drag-and-drop website builder, one-click WordPress installation, and a variety of hosting options, including shared, VPS, and dedicated servers.

DreamHost: offers a range of hosting solutions, including shared hosting, managed WordPress hosting, VPS, and dedicated servers. They focus on providing reliable performance, solid security features, and extensive developer tools.

WP Engine: WP Engine specializes in managed WordPress hosting, catering specifically to WordPress websites. They offer robust security, automatic backups, staging environments, and excellent customer support tailored to WordPress users.

When choosing a web hosting provider, consider the following factors:

Hosting Plans: Evaluate the available hosting options and choose the one that best suits your website's needs, considering factors like expected traffic, storage requirements, and scalability.

Pricing and Features: Compare pricing structures and features offered by different providers. Pay attention to factors such as storage capacity, bandwidth, email accounts, website builders, and customer support.

Reliability and Uptime: Look for providers with high uptime guarantees to ensure that your website remains accessible to visitors. A reliable hosting provider will have robust infrastructure and backup systems in place.

Customer Support: Check the availability and quality of customer support options. Look for providers offering 24/7 support via various channels, such as live chat, phone, and email.

User-Friendly Control Panel: Consider the ease of use of the hosting provider's control panel, as it will be your primary interface for managing your website, domains, email accounts, and other settings.

By carefully evaluating these factors and selecting a reputable web hosting provider, you can ensure a solid foundation for your website's success.

In the next chapter, we will explore the process of setting up and configuring your website using popular content management systems like WordPress.

(4) Setting Up and Configuring Your Website

After successfully registering your domain and acquiring web hosting, the next crucial step in your website's journey is configuring the Domain Name System (DNS) settings for your domain. DNS is a fundamental component of the internet, responsible for translating human-readable domain names into the IP addresses that computers use to locate your website. In this comprehensive guide, we will walk you through the process of configuring DNS and provide insights into the concept of propagation time, a critical aspect of DNS management.

Accessing DNS Settings

To configure DNS for your domain, you must access the DNS settings associated with your domain. Here's how you can do it:

Log in to your domain registrar's website: This is the platform where you initially registered your domain.

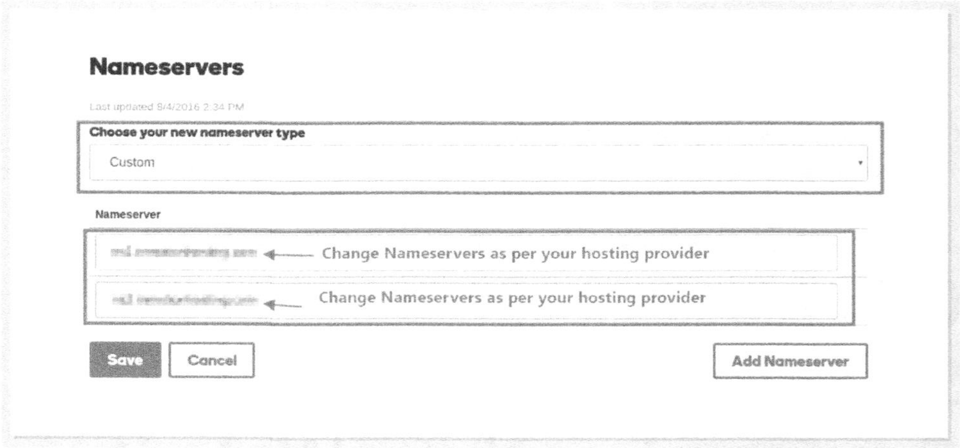

At the end of this book, you will find supporting materials, such as links to high-resolution images and much more.

Locate the domain management section: You should find a dedicated area or domain settings for the specific domain you wish to configure.

Find options like "DNS Management," "Name Servers," or "DNS Settings." The precise terminology may vary depending on your registrar, but these labels typically point to the right place.

Name Servers

Name servers are the machines that store the DNS records for your domain. By default, your domain registrar assigns its own name servers to your domain. However, if you've obtained web hosting, you will need to update the name servers to point to your hosting provider's name servers.

Obtain the name server information: Your web hosting provider should supply you with two or more name server addresses.

In the DNS settings of your domain registrar: Locate the name server fields.

Replace the existing name server addresses: Replace the default values with those provided by your web hosting provider. **Save the changes.**

DNS Propagation

DNS propagation refers to the time it takes for the updated DNS information to propagate across the vast expanse of the internet. During this propagation period, various DNS servers worldwide update their records with the new DNS information. It's essential to understand that propagation is not instantaneous and can take anywhere from a few minutes to as long as 48 hours or more.

During this transitional period, some users may still be directed to the old DNS records, while others will see the updated information. This variance occurs because different DNS servers update at different intervals. Patience is crucial while waiting for the changes to take full effect.

Verifying DNS Configuration

To ensure that your DNS configuration is correct, you can conduct the following checks:

Use DNS Lookup Tools: Numerous online tools allow you to perform DNS lookups for your domain. Enter your domain name and verify if the returned information matches your updated DNS settings.

Clear DNS Cache: Your computer and internet service provider may have cached the old DNS information. Clearing the DNS cache can help retrieve the updated records. Instructions for clearing the cache vary based on your operating system.

For Your Information

Additionally, you can check the status of your website's propagation by searching online for "Site Propagation." Several websites offer free tools for checking your DNS information. Simply enter your domain name and verify that your NS (Name Server) is updated.

Additional DNS Configurations

Besides updating name servers, you might need to configure other DNS records based on your website's requirements. Common DNS records include:

A Record: Associates your domain name with the IP address of your web hosting server. This record directs visitors to the correct server when they enter your domain.

CNAME Record: Allows you to create subdomains or alias domains that point to another domain or server.

MX Record: Specifies the mail server responsible for handling email delivery for your domain.

SPF Record: Helps prevent email spoofing and verifies that emails sent from your domain are legitimate.

TXT Record: Allows you to add custom text-based information to your DNS records, often used for verification or providing additional domain details.

Consult your web hosting provider's documentation or support resources to understand the specific DNS records you may need to configure.

Once you've completed the DNS configuration and the changes have fully propagated, your domain will be correctly connected to your web hosting. It's essential to periodically review and update your DNS settings as needed, especially when making changes to your hosting provider or server configuration. Proper DNS management ensures that your website remains accessible, secure, and performs optimally for your visitors.

(5) Installing WordPress on Your Web Hosting

With your domain configured, DNS settings in place, and web hosting secured, it's time to embark on the journey of installing WordPress. This renowned content management system fuels millions of websites across the globe. In this chapter, we'll take you through the step-by-step process of setting up WordPress on your web hosting.

Automatic Installation (Easy way)

Automatic installation of WordPress refers to the process of installing WordPress on your web hosting server using automated installation tools or scripts provided by hosting providers. Many hosting companies offer one-click installation options for WordPress, which simplify the installation process and eliminate the need for manual configuration. If you need some help, your web hosting can help you.

At the end of this book, you will find supporting materials, such as links to high-resolution images and much more.

Here's how automatic installation of WordPress typically works:

Choose WordPress as Your CMS (Content Management System): When signing up for a web hosting service, you may be asked to select the content management system (CMS) you want to install. Choose WordPress from the available options.

Select Installation Location: During the setup process, you will need to specify the directory or subdomain where you want to install WordPress. You can choose to install it in the root directory (e.g., yourdomain.com) or in a subdirectory (e.g., yourdomain.com/blog).

Provide Administrative Details: You will be asked to enter the administrative details for your WordPress installation, including the site title, username, password, and email address. These details will be used to log into your WordPress dashboard.

Run the Installation: Once you have provided the necessary information, click on the "Install" or "Setup" button. The hosting provider's automated script will handle the installation process for you.

Wait for the Installation to Complete: The automated installation script will configure the necessary files, set up the database, and install WordPress on your server. You may need to wait for a few moments while the installation process is completed.

Access Your WordPress Dashboard: After the installation is finished, you will be provided with the URL to access your WordPress dashboard. Simply click on the provided link or enter your website's URL followed by "/wp-admin" to log in.

Automatic installation of WordPress is convenient for users who are less experienced with manual configuration or prefer a hassle-free setup process. It streamlines the installation steps and ensures that the necessary files and database are set up correctly. However, it's important to note that the available options and user interfaces may vary among hosting providers, so the exact steps and terminology used during the automatic installation process may differ slightly.

Manual Installations

Manual installation of WordPress refers to the process of installing WordPress on your web hosting server manually, without using automated installation tools or scripts provided by hosting providers. While many hosting companies offer one-click installation options

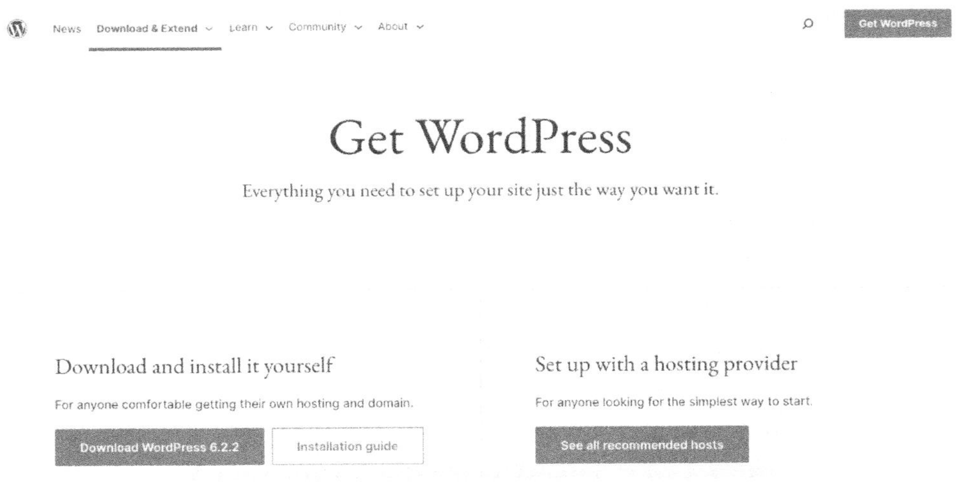

News Download & Extend Learn Community About Get WordPress

Get WordPress

Everything you need to set up your site just the way you want it.

Download and install it yourself

For anyone comfortable getting their own hosting and domain.

Download WordPress 6.2.2 Installation guide

Set up with a hosting provider

For anyone looking for the simplest way to start.

See all recommended hosts

for WordPress, some users prefer to manually install WordPress for various reasons, such as having more control over the installation process or troubleshooting specific issues.

Here are the basic steps involved in manually installing WordPress:

Download the WordPress Installation Package: Visit the official WordPress website at wordpress.org and download the latest version of WordPress. (https://wordpress.org/download

Prepare the Files: Extract the contents of the downloaded WordPress package on your computer. This will create a folder containing all the necessary files for installation.

Create a Database: Before proceeding with the installation, create a MySQL database and assign a user to it. You can typically do this through your hosting control panel or using a tool like phpMyAdmin.

For Your Information

A web hosting database is a foundational component of modern web development and online applications. It serves as a structured collection of data, meticulously organized and stored within a computer system or server. The purpose of a database is to efficiently manage and manipulate large volumes of information, enabling easy access, retrieval, and modification of data for a myriad of purposes, from dynamic websites to complex business applications.

To create a database, you can follow these general steps:

Access your web hosting control panel: Log in to your web hosting account and navigate to the control panel. The control panel may vary depending on the hosting provider you are using.

Locate the database section: In the control panel, look for the section related to databases. It is usually labeled as "Databases," "MySQL Databases," or something similar.

Create a new database: Within the database section, there should be an option to create a new database. Click on it, and you will be prompted to enter a name for your new database. Choose a name that is descriptive and easy to remember.

Set up database credentials: After creating the database, you will need to set up a username and password to access and manage the database. These credentials will be used in your website's configuration file to establish a connection with the database.

Assign privileges to the user: Once the database user is created, you will need to assign appropriate privileges to the user for accessing and modifying the database. Typically, the user will require at least "All Privileges" to effectively manage the database.

Save the database details: Take note of the database name, username, password, and the host (usually localhost). These details will be necessary when configuring your website or any applications that need to connect to the database.

Configure your website/application: Depending on the specific website or application you are working with, you will need to locate the configuration file. This file is often named something like "wp-config.php" for WordPress or "config.php" for custom-built websites. Inside the configuration file, you will find settings to enter the database details you previously noted down.

Test the database connection: After configuring the database details in your website/application, it's essential to test the database connection. You can do this by visiting your website or launching your application and ensuring that it can successfully connect to the database.

Configure the wp-config.php File: In the WordPress folder you extracted earlier, locate the file named "wp-config-sample.php" and rename it to "wp-config.php". Open this file in a text editor and enter your database information, including the database name, username, password, and host. (You can check how to access this file using text editors in the next Subtitle).

Configuring the wp-config.php file in both Mac and Windows involves similar steps, although the specific methods may vary slightly. Here's a general guide on how to configure the wp-config.php file on both platforms:

Locate the wp-config.php File:

On Mac: Open the Finder and navigate to the root folder of your WordPress installation. The wp-config.php file should be located in the root directory.

On Windows: Open the File Explorer and navigate to the root folder of your WordPress installation. The wp-config.php file should be located in the root directory.

Open the wp-config.php File:

On Mac: Right-click on the wp-config.php file and select "Open With" from the context menu. Choose a text editor like TextEdit or Sublime Text to open the file.

On Windows: Right-click on the wp-config.php file and select "Open With" from the context menu. Choose a text editor like Notepad or Sublime Text to open the file.

Edit the Configuration Constants:

```
define('DB_NAME', 'database_name');
define('DB_USER', 'username');
define('DB_PASSWORD', 'password');
define('DB_HOST', 'localhost');
```

Database Settings: Locate the section in the wp-config.php file where the database settings are defined. You'll find lines similar to the following:

Replace 'database_name', 'username', 'password', and 'localhost' with the appropriate values for your MySQL database. Consult your hosting provider or database administrator for the correct credentials.

Authentication Unique Keys and Salts: Look for the section containing the authentication unique keys and salts. These lines start with define('AUTH_KEY', define('SECURE_AUTH_KEY', define('LOGGED_IN_KEY', and so on. These keys and

```
define('AUTH_KEY',         'put your unique phrase here');
define('SECURE_AUTH_KEY',  'put your unique phrase here');
define('LOGGED_IN_KEY',    'put your unique phrase here');
define('NONCE_KEY',        'put your unique phrase here');
```

salts enhance the security of your WordPress installation.

Visit the WordPress Secret Key Generator to generate unique phrases. Replace the existing phrases with the newly generated ones.

Save and Close the File:

On Mac: After making the necessary changes, save the wp-config.php file and close the text editor.

On Windows: Save the wp-config.php file and close the text editor.

After configuring the wp-config.php file, you can proceed with the installation or use of your WordPress website. The file contains important configuration settings, including database credentials and security keys, which are crucial for the proper functioning of your WordPress installation.

Note: When editing the wp-config.php file, exercise caution to avoid accidentally modifying or deleting any critical code. Make a backup of the original file before making any changes, as it can help restore the original configuration in case of errors or issues.

Upload WordPress Files: Connect to your web hosting server using an FTP client or the file manager provided by your hosting control panel. Upload the entire WordPress folder (containing the extracted files) to the desired location on your server. This is usually the root directory or a subdirectory where you want to install WordPress.

Here is a list of popular FTP (File Transfer Protocol) software:

FileZilla: FileZilla is a free and open-source FTP client available for Windows, macOS, and Linux. It has a user-friendly interface and supports FTP, FTPS, and SFTP.

WinSCP: WinSCP is a free and open-source FTP client for Windows. It offers both an FTP client and an SFTP client with a dual-pane interface and supports secure file transfers.

Cyberduck: Cyberduck is a free and open-source FTP client available for Windows and macOS. It supports FTP, SFTP, WebDAV, and other protocols and provides a modern and intuitive interface.

Transmit: Transmit is a popular FTP client for macOS. It offers a clean and user-friendly interface, supports FTP, SFTP, WebDAV, and Amazon S3, and includes features like syncing and file transfer queuing.

CuteFTP: CuteFTP is a commercial FTP client available for Windows. It provides an easy-to-use interface and supports FTP, FTPS, SFTP, and WebDAV.

Fetch: Fetch is an FTP client designed for macOS. It offers a straightforward interface, supports FTP and SFTP, and includes features like automatic resuming of interrupted transfers.

Core FTP: Core FTP is a free FTP client for Windows. It supports FTP, FTPS, SSH/SFTP, and includes features like file compression and encryption.

FireFTP: FireFTP is a free FTP client that runs as a browser extension on Mozilla Firefox. It provides a simple and intuitive interface and supports FTP and SFTP.

SmartFTP: SmartFTP is a commercial FTP client available for Windows. It offers an extensive range of features, including FTP, FTPS, SFTP, WebDAV, and remote file editing.

lftp: lftp is a command-line FTP client available for Windows, macOS, and Linux. It supports FTP, FTPS, and SFTP and offers a rich set of command-line options for automation.

To connect your website with FTP software, you'll need the following information:

FTP Host/Server: This is the hostname or IP address of your web server. It is usually provided by your web hosting provider. Look in your web hosting control panel. You can ask the web hosting support for help.

FTP Username and Password: These are the credentials used to access your FTP account. They are usually provided by your web hosting provider or can be created within your hosting control panel.

Once you have this information, follow these general steps to connect your website using FTP software (using FileZilla as an example):

1. Download and install the FTP software of your choice (e.g., FileZilla, WinSCP, Cyberduck).
2. Launch the FTP software and open the program.
3. Enter the FTP Host/Server, FTP Username, and FTP Password in the appropriate fields. Make sure to choose the correct protocol (FTP, FTPS, SFTP) based on the server settings.
4. Set the Port to the default FTP port (usually 21) or use the one provided by your web hosting provider.

5. Click the "Connect" or "Quick Connect" button to establish a connection to the FTP server.

6. Once connected, you will see the files and folders on your web server in the software's interface, typically divided into two panels: the local files (your computer) and the remote files (web server).

7. You can now navigate through the directories on your web server and manage your website files by uploading, downloading, deleting, or editing them as needed.

It's important to note that the exact steps and interface may vary slightly depending on the FTP software you're using. However, the general process remains the same. If you encounter any difficulties, consult the documentation or support resources provided by the specific FTP software you're using for further guidance.

Run the Installation Script: Once the files are uploaded, open a web browser and enter your website's URL (e.g., www.yourdomain.com) to start the WordPress installation process. If you installed WordPress in a subdirectory, include the subdirectory name in the URL (e.g., www.yourdomain.com/subdirectory).

Complete the Installation: Follow the on-screen instructions to complete the WordPress installation. You will be asked to provide the site title, username, password, and email address for your WordPress website. After providing the necessary information, click on the "Install WordPress" or "Run Installation" button.

Access Your WordPress Dashboard: Once the installation is complete, you can log into your WordPress dashboard by visiting your website's URL followed by "/wp-admin" (e.g., www.yourdomain.com/wp-admin). Enter your username and password to access the admin area.

Manual installation of WordPress requires a basic understanding of web servers, FTP, and databases. It gives you more flexibility and control over the installation process, but it can also be more time-consuming and may require additional troubleshooting if any issues arise.

Text Editors and Development Tools for Mac and Windows (For Manual Installation)

To configure the wp-config.php direct in your web host using Mac or Windows, you can use various text editors and development tools. There are several text editors. You can choose one of your preference. Some text editors you can work directly from your web hosting, connecting your website.

TextEdit: TextEdit is a default text editor included with macOS. It provides basic text editing capabilities and can be used to open and modify the wp-config.php file.

Sublime Text: Sublime Text is a powerful text editor with a sleek user interface. It offers advanced features such as syntax highlighting, code snippets, and multiple cursors, making it a favorite among developers.

Atom: Atom is an open-source text editor developed by GitHub. It is highly customizable and comes with a range of features and packages that enhance the editing experience for web development.

Nova: is a popular code editor specifically designed for macOS. It is a powerful and feature-rich application that provides developers with a seamless coding experience. Nova offers a wide range of tools and functionalities to streamline the development process and enhance productivity.

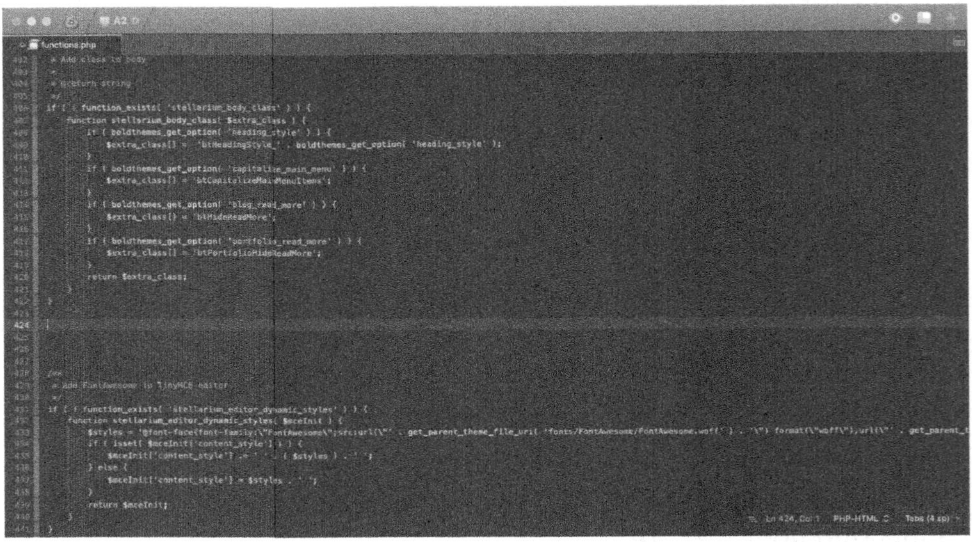

Notepad: Notepad is a simple text editor that comes pre-installed with Windows. While it lacks advanced features, it can still be used to edit the wp-config.php file.

Sublime Text: Sublime Text is available for both Mac and Windows and provides a consistent editing experience across platforms. It offers powerful features that make working with code efficient and enjoyable.

Visual Studio Code: Visual Studio Code (VS Code) is a popular choice among developers. It is a free, open-source code editor with a wide range of extensions and integrations that enhance productivity.

These are just a few examples of the software available for editing the wp-config.php file. Ultimately, you can choose any text editor that you are comfortable with and that supports editing plain text files. The key is to have a reliable editor that allows you to make the necessary modifications to the file and save it correctly.

A - To access your web host, you typically need to follow these steps:

Obtain the Host's Control Panel URL: Your web hosting provider should provide you with the URL or web address of their control panel. This control panel is where you can manage various aspects of your web hosting account.

Open a Web Browser: Launch your preferred web browser, such as Google Chrome, Mozilla Firefox, or Safari.

Enter the Control Panel URL: In the address bar of your web browser, type or paste the URL provided by your hosting provider for accessing the control panel.

Press Enter: Hit the Enter key or click the Go button to initiate the connection.

Authenticate: Depending on your hosting provider and control panel software, you may be prompted to enter your username and password. Enter the credentials associated with your web hosting account. If you don't have these details or have forgotten them, contact your hosting provider for assistance.

Access the Control Panel: After successful authentication, you will be logged into the control panel of your web host. The control panel provides various tools and options to manage your web hosting account, such as managing domains, setting up email accounts, configuring databases, and more.

Explore and Manage Your Web Hosting Account: Once inside the control panel, you can navigate through the available features and options to perform tasks specific to your web hosting needs. This may include uploading files, installing applications, creating databases, managing FTP accounts, and other administrative tasks related to your website or web application.

B - To access your web host using an app like Nova, you can follow these steps:

Install and Launch Nova: Start by installing the Nova app on your Mac computer and launch it. Nova is a code editor specifically designed for macOS. You can use any code editor, as a previous list.

Open a New Project: In Nova, go to the "File" menu and select "New Project" or use the keyboard shortcut (Command + Shift + N) to create a new project.

Configure Project Settings: In the project configuration window, provide the necessary details to set up the connection to your web host. This typically includes:

- Project Name: Enter a name for your project to identify it within Nova.
- Remote Server Type: Select the appropriate protocol based on your web host's configuration (e.g., FTP, SFTP).
- Server Address or Host: Enter the server address or domain name provided by your hosting provider.

- Username and Password: Provide the FTP/SFTP login credentials associated with your web hosting account. These credentials are usually different from your control panel login.

- Port (if required): If your hosting provider uses a non-standard port for FTP/SFTP, enter the appropriate port number.

Test and Save the Connection: Once you've entered the project settings, click on the "Test Connection" or similar button in Nova to establish a connection to your web host. If the connection is successful, you can save the project for future use.

Access Your Web Host: After saving the project, Nova will display the file tree of your web host's directory structure. You can navigate through the directories, view and edit files, upload new files, or download existing ones.

Manage Files and Make Changes: Using Nova, you can easily edit HTML, CSS, JavaScript, and other web files directly on your web host. The app provides a convenient interface with features like syntax highlighting, code suggestions, and version control integration.

By using an app like Nova, you can access your web host and manage your website files more efficiently, enhancing your development workflow and productivity.

Please note that the steps may slightly vary depending on the version of Nova you are using. Consult the app's documentation or reach out to their support if you encounter any issues during the setup process.

(6)
Accessing Your WordPress Admin Panel

In this exciting chapter, I'll guide you through the process of accessing your WordPress Admin Panel. This is where all the magic happens, where you can take control of your website's settings, content, and much more. So, let's get started on this journey of empowerment and discovery.

The WordPress Admin Panel, also known as the WordPress Dashboard, is the backend interface of a WordPress website where site administrators and authorized users manage and control various aspects of the site. It provides a user-friendly and intuitive interface for managing content, customizing the site's appearance, configuring settings, and monitoring site performance.

Locating the Admin Panel

To access your WordPress Admin Panel, you need to know its location. Simply add "/wp-admin" to the end of your website's URL (e.g., www.yourwebsite.com/wp-admin). This will take you to the login page of your Admin Panel.

Logging in

On the login page, you will need to enter your credentials: your username and password. These are the details you set up during the installation of WordPress or were provided by your website administrator. Make sure to enter the correct information to gain access to your Admin Panel.

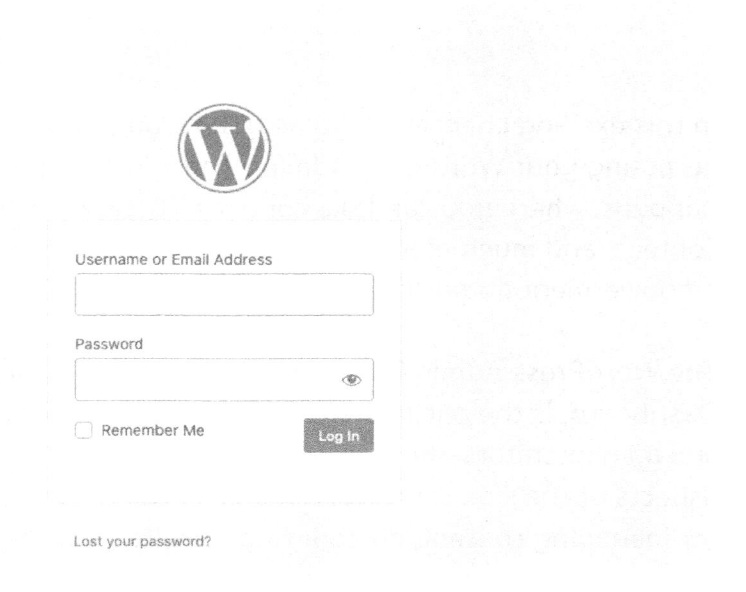

Exploring the Admin Panel Interface

Once you have successfully logged in, you will be greeted by the Admin Panel interface. This is your control center, where you can manage your website's content, appearance, settings, and more. Let's take a closer look at some of the key elements within the Admin Panel:

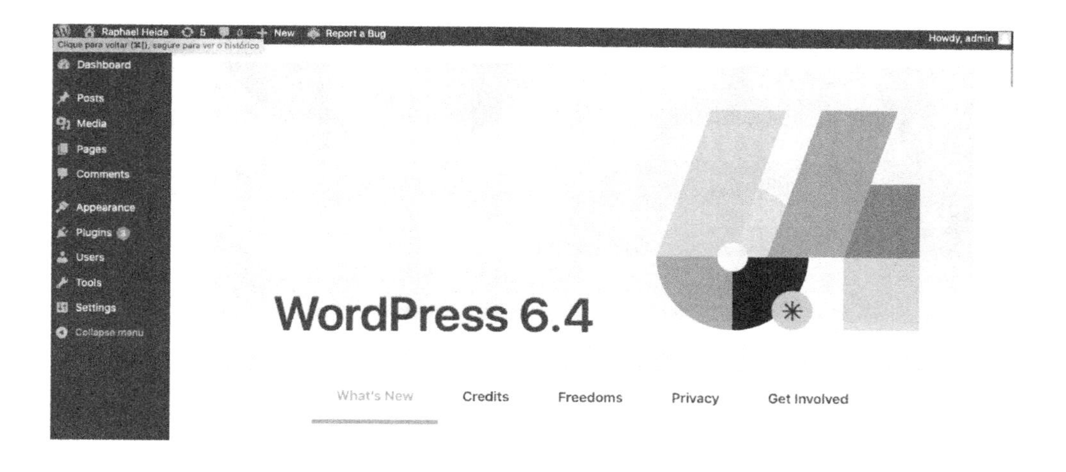

Dashboard: The Dashboard is the first screen you see after logging in. It provides an overview of your site's activity, including recent posts, comments, and statistics. It serves as a hub from which you can access various sections of the Admin Panel.

Menu: Located on the left-hand side, the menu provides quick navigation to different areas of your Admin Panel. It consists of options such as Posts, Pages, Media, Appearance, Plugins, and Settings. Each option represents a specific aspect of your website that you can manage.

Toolbar: The Toolbar, located at the top of the screen, provides quick access to commonly used features. It allows you to create new posts, view your website's front-end, access your profile, and more. The Toolbar is there to make your workflow more efficient.

Welcome to WordPress panel always shows the last WordPress version.

Welcome to WordPress!

Learn more about the 6.4 version.

Navigating the Admin Panel

To explore different sections of the Admin Panel, simply click on the corresponding menu option. For example, clicking on "Posts" will take you to the section where you can create, edit, and manage your blog posts. Each section has its own set of sub-menus and options, allowing you to fine-tune your website according to your preferences.

For Your Information

The WordPress Admin Panel, often referred to as the Dashboard, is the digital cockpit and command center for your website. It's the place where you, as the website owner or administrator, take control of all aspects of your online presence. Whether you're a seasoned WordPress user or just beginning your web development journey, understanding the ins and outs of the Admin Panel is crucial to effectively manage and maintain your website.

(7)
Difference Between Posts and Pages on WordPress

In this chapter, we'll delve into the core distinctions between posts and pages. Gaining a clear understanding of these differences is paramount for anyone looking to harness the full potential of their WordPress website.

Posts and pages are the building blocks of your website's content, each serving a unique purpose. This chapter will equip you with the knowledge to create, manage, and organize your content more effectively. So, without further ado, let's dive into the world of WordPress and uncover the distinctive characteristics that define posts and pages, empowering you to make the most out of your web presence.

Posts: Dynamic Content for Blogging

Posts are the lifeblood of a WordPress blog. They are designed for regularly updated content, such as articles, news, and stories. Posts play a crucial role in maintaining an active blog and providing fresh, regularly updated content for visitors. They are suitable for publishing articles, news updates, personal reflections, tutorials, and other types of blog entries.

Here's what you need to know about posts:

Adding a New Post: To create a new post, navigate to the WordPress Admin Panel and click on "Posts" in the menu. From there, select "Add New." You'll be directed to the post editor, where you can write and format your content.

Deleting a Post: If you want to remove a post, go to the "Posts" section in the Admin Panel. Find the post you wish to delete and hover over its title. A set of options will appear, including the "Trash" option. Click on it to send the post to the trash. Remember, you can recover deleted posts from the trash within a certain period before they are permanently deleted.

Updating a Post: To update an existing post, go to the "Posts" section, locate the post you want to edit, and click on its title. This will open the post editor, where you can make changes to the content, update the title, add or remove images, and modify any other element. Once you're done, remember to save or publish your changes.

Post Formats: WordPress offers various post formats, such as standard, gallery, video, audio, quote, and more. These formats allow you to present your content in different styles, enhancing the visual appeal and engagement of your posts. You can select the desired format within the post editor.

Pages: Static Content for Essential Information

Unlike posts, pages are meant for static content that doesn't require frequent updates. Pages are ideal for creating timeless information, such as your About page, Contact page, or Services page. Let's delve into the specifics:

Adding a New Page: To create a new page, go to the Admin Panel and click on "Pages" in the menu. Choose "Add New" to access the page editor. Similar to creating a post, you can input your content, format it, and add media as needed.

Deleting a Page: To remove a page, navigate to the "Pages" section in the Admin Panel. Locate the page you wish to delete, hover over its title, and click on the "Trash" option. Deleted pages are stored in the trash, allowing you to restore them if needed.

Updating a Page: To update an existing page, go to the "Pages" section, find the page you want to edit, and click on its title. The page editor will open, enabling you to modify the content, update the page title, change the layout, or add new elements. Don't forget to save your changes after editing.

Page Templates: WordPress provides various page templates that determine the layout and design of your pages. These templates allow you to create different styles for specific pages, such as full-width pages, landing pages, or contact forms. You can choose a page template while editing or creating a page.

(8)
Using Gutenberg on WordPress

Gutenberg is a modern block-based content editor for WordPress. It was introduced as a significant change to the WordPress editor, starting with WordPress version 5.0. Gutenberg replaces the classic WordPress editor with a more intuitive and flexible way to create and edit content.

The key feature of Gutenberg is the concept of "blocks." Instead of a single, large text editor, content is divided into smaller blocks. Each block can be customized individually, making it easier to create complex and visually appealing layouts. Gutenberg offers a wide range of pre-built blocks for common content elements like paragraphs, headings, images, videos, buttons, and more. Users can also create custom blocks or install additional block plugins to extend functionality.

This block-based approach simplifies content creation, as users can add, arrange, and style content elements in a visual and user-friendly way. It's especially helpful for those who may not have extensive technical or design skills.

Gutenberg has had a significant impact on WordPress, making it easier for users to create and manage content while providing more control over the visual presentation of their websites. While it represented a substantial change when initially introduced, it has since become an integral part of WordPress, and many users have embraced its capabilities for creating dynamic and engaging content.

Get ready to unlock your creativity and take your WordPress experience to the next level.

Understanding Gutenberg: What Is It All About?

Gutenberg, a transformative addition to the WordPress platform, represents a major shift in the way users create, edit, and manage content on their websites. This innovative editor replaces the traditional WordPress editor with a block-based system, fundamentally altering the content creation experience.

In the Gutenberg editor, the concept of "blocks" takes center stage. Rather than the conventional single text field, content is now constructed using individual, versatile blocks, each designed to serve a specific purpose. These blocks encompass a wide range of content elements, offering users the freedom to craft their posts and pages with precision and creativity.

You can start with the basics, such as text paragraphs and headings, which are the fundamental building blocks of any content piece. Gutenberg also allows for easy integration of media, such as images and videos, making your content visually engaging. Additionally, you can incorporate more advanced blocks, like image galleries, pull quotes, and embedded social media posts, with minimal effort.

One of the most exciting aspects of Gutenberg is its compatibility with custom-designed blocks through the use of plugins. This means you can extend the functionality of your editor by adding specialized blocks that cater to your specific needs. Whether it's a block for showcasing your latest products, integrating a booking system, or creating interactive forms, there's a plugin-generated block for virtually any purpose.

Beyond the creative freedom it offers, Gutenberg is also the hub where you write and structure your posts or pages. Its user-friendly interface simplifies the content creation process, allowing you to focus on your message rather than the technicalities of formatting and layout. Each block can be individually customized, offering control over every detail of your content, from text styling to multimedia placement.

In essence, Gutenberg is more than just a content editor; it's a comprehensive tool that empowers users to express their ideas with precision, style, and efficiency. This transition from the classic editor to Gutenberg has not only modernized the WordPress content creation experience but has also opened new horizons for innovative web design and user-friendly content management. As a result, it has been widely embraced by the WordPress community and continues to play a pivotal role in shaping the future of content creation on the web.

Getting Started with Gutenberg

To start using Gutenberg, ensure that you have the latest version of WordPress installed. If you're already running WordPress 5.0 or higher, Gutenberg is already integrated into your setup. Here's how to create a new post or page with Gutenberg:

- Log in to your WordPress Admin Panel.

- Click on "Posts" or "Pages" in the sidebar menu, depending on where you want to create your content.

- Click on the "Add New" button to start a new post or page.

Exploring the Gutenberg Interface

Once you've entered the Gutenberg editor, you'll notice a clean and intuitive interface designed for seamless content creation. Let's explore the key components:

Block Toolbar: When you select a block, a toolbar appears above it. This toolbar allows you to perform various actions related to that block, such as formatting text, adding links, adjusting alignment, and more.

Block Navigation: On the right side of the editor, you'll find the block navigation panel. This panel displays all the blocks within your content, making it easy to navigate and edit specific blocks.

Block Library: To add a new block, click on the "+" icon located at the top left corner of the editor. This opens the block library, where you can choose from a wide range of available blocks. You can also search for specific blocks or use the "Most Used" or "Reusable" block categories.

Document Settings: Access the document settings by clicking on the gear icon located in the top-right corner of the editor. Here, you can set the post or page title, featured image, categories, tags, and more.

Working with Blocks

Blocks are the building blocks of your content in Gutenberg. Here are some essential tips for effectively working with blocks:

Adding Blocks: To add a new block, click on the "+" icon and select the desired block type from the library. Alternatively, you can use the slash (/) command in the editor to search for and insert blocks.

These blocks are the fundamental building components of content in the block-based editing system. Each block represents a specific type of content or functionality, and you can arrange and customize them individually to create rich and dynamic layouts on your website.

Rearranging Blocks: You can easily rearrange blocks by clicking and dragging them up or down. This allows you to structure your content precisely the way you want it.

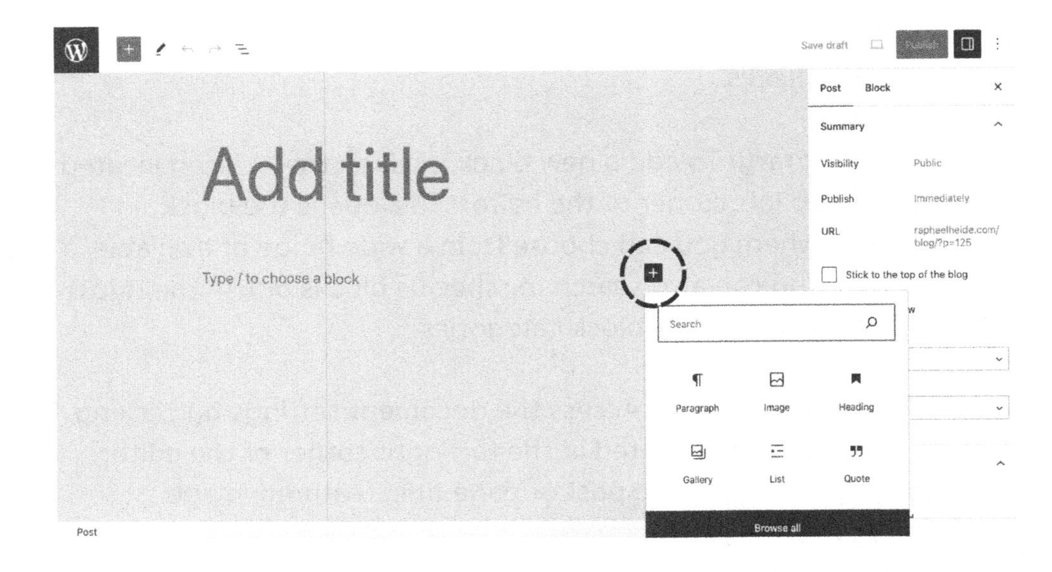

At the end of this book, you will find supporting materials, such as links to high-resolution images and much more.

Block Settings: Each block has its own set of settings that you can access by clicking on the block and selecting the block-specific options from the toolbar or block settings panel.

Block Styling: Gutenberg provides block-level styling options to customize the appearance of individual blocks. You can adjust colors, fonts, sizes, and more using the block settings or the global styles panel.

Saving and Reusing Blocks: Gutenberg allows you to save blocks as reusable blocks. This feature is handy when you want to reuse a block across different posts or pages. To save a block, select it and click on the three-dot menu in the block toolbar. Then, choose "Add to Reusable Blocks."

Experimenting with Advanced Features

Gutenberg offers advanced features and integrations that enhance your content creation experience. Here are a few notable features to explore:

Full-Site Editing: With Full-Site Editing, you can customize your entire website using Gutenberg. This feature enables you to modify headers, footers, sidebars, and other global elements using blocks.

Plugins and Block Patterns: Extend Gutenberg's functionality by installing plugins that provide additional blocks and block patterns. These plugins offer a vast array of design options and customizations.

Collaboration and Revisions: Gutenberg facilitates collaboration by allowing multiple users to edit content simultaneously. It also provides a revision history, enabling you to track changes and restore previous versions if needed.

You can save your post or page as a draft or publish.

Blocks can encompass a wide range of content and features, such as:

Paragraph Block: For text and regular content.

Heading Block: For creating headings and subheadings.

Image Block: To add images to your content.

Gallery Block: To create image galleries.

Quote Block: For displaying quotations or highlighting text.

List Block: For creating lists, both ordered and unordered.

Button Block: To add call-to-action buttons.

Embeds: These blocks allow you to easily embed content from external sources like YouTube, Twitter, and other websites.

Custom HTML Block: For adding custom HTML code.

Custom Blocks: You can also create or install custom blocks through plugins, which can add various functionalities like contact forms, accordions, testimonials, and more.

We will the more about blocks in "Posts and Pages: More Functions" chapter.

(9)
Posts and Pages Summary

In this concise chapter, we'll explore the fundamental elements of WordPress posts and pages. Understanding these basics will empower you to create and manage content effectively on your website. Let's get started!

Posts and Pages Summary are localized on right hand:

Visibility

When creating a post or page, you have the option to set its visibility. By default, posts and pages are set to "Public," meaning they are visible to everyone. However, you can also choose to make them "Private" so that only logged-in users with the appropriate permissions can view them.

Additionally, you can mark posts or pages as "Password Protected," requiring visitors to enter a password to access the content.

Publish

The "Publish" meta box within WordPress is a powerful tool that grants you precise control over when your content becomes accessible to the public. It is a fundamental aspect of content management and is essential for strategizing and optimizing your content release schedule.

At its core, the "Publish" meta box empowers you with the ability to dictate the exact moment when a post or page should be made available to your audience. You have the flexibility to select a specific date and time for publication, ensuring that your content goes live at the most opportune moment. This level of control is invaluable, especially when timing is critical for the relevance and impact of your content.

One of the most common scenarios is the option to publish a post immediately. This is ideal for content that is time-sensitive or for situations where you're eager to share your latest insights, updates, or news with your audience without delay. With just a click, your content can be instantly available to the public.

However, the "Publish" meta box offers a far more advanced and strategic capability: the ability to schedule posts for future publication. This feature is particularly valuable for content creators and publishers who wish to plan and organize their content well in advance. By specifying a future date and time for publication, you can maintain a consistent content schedule, even if you're not actively publishing posts in real-time.

Scheduled posts can be a game-changer for a variety of purposes. For instance, it allows you to maintain a steady stream of fresh content, even during periods when you may be busy or unavailable. It's a vital tool for bloggers, news outlets, and anyone with a content calendar that spans days, weeks, or even months. Scheduling posts ensures that your website remains active and engaging, even when you're not actively present.

This feature is also particularly advantageous for international audiences. You can plan your content to be published at times that align with the peak activity of your target audience, regardless of time zone differences. This level of precision can significantly impact your content's reach and engagement.

URL

Each post and page in WordPress have a unique URL, also known as the permalink. Permalinks play a crucial role in Search Engine Optimization (SEO) and user experience. WordPress allows you to customize the structure of your permalinks, making them more descriptive and user-friendly. We will talk about SEO in this book.

Author

WordPress enables multiple users to contribute to a website, and each post or page can be attributed to a specific author. The author's name is displayed alongside the content, providing transparency and credit to the respective contributor. This feature is especially valuable for websites with multiple authors or guest writers.

Categories

Categories help organize your posts into broader topics or sections. They act as a hierarchical grouping system, allowing visitors to navigate and explore related content easily. When creating a post, you can assign it to one or more categories to ensure proper classification and better user navigation.

Tags

In the intricate web of content organization within WordPress, tags emerge as a highly valuable and nuanced tool. They might appear similar to categories at first glance, both serving the purpose of classifying and organizing content, but upon closer examination, tags reveal their unique and intricate role in content management.

Unlike categories, which often represent broader and hierarchical classifications, tags offer a more granular and detailed level of classification. They are like the fine brushstrokes on a canvas, the precise and specific descriptors that help paint a more detailed picture of the content's focus. Tags, in essence, are the refined keywords or topics that intimately connect with a post's core subject matter.

The beauty of tags lies in their non-hierarchical nature. While categories often establish a structured and hierarchical framework for content, tags operate in a more fluid and flexible manner. A post can have multiple tags, each representing different aspects or facets of the content. This adaptability allows for a richer and more diverse content landscape, as one piece of content can be associated with a variety of related keywords or topics.

Why do tags matter? Their significance becomes apparent when we consider content discoverability and the reader's journey through your website. Tags play a pivotal role in guiding visitors to content that aligns with their interests or queries. When a reader stumbles upon a post and finds it intriguing or informative, they may want more of the same. This is where tags shine, as they create pathways to related posts that share similar tags.

Tags enhance the visitor's experience by making it easier for them to explore related content effortlessly. When a visitor clicks on a tag associated with a post they're reading, they're presented with a curated selection of other posts that delve into the same subject matter, thus encouraging deeper engagement and exploration of your website.

In a broader context, tags have a significant impact on SEO (Search Engine Optimization). When search engines crawl your website, they use tags to understand the context and relevance of your content. Properly tagged content can result in better search engine rankings, as it helps search engines match your posts with relevant search queries.

Featured Image

In the realm of content creation and digital storytelling, the featured image takes center stage as a pivotal visual component of your WordPress posts and pages. Often referred to as the "post thumbnail," it plays a critical role in capturing the essence of your content, offering readers a sneak peek into the world you're about to unfold. This visual representation stands as a powerful tool for making a memorable first impression, not only on your website but also across various digital platforms.

The featured image is more than just a visual afterthought; it's a deliberate choice that can shape the way your content is perceived and received by your audience. Its significance extends beyond the confines of your post or page, as it often takes the spotlight on archive pages, social media shares, and even within the post itself. With so many potential touchpoints, the featured image is a cornerstone in crafting a compelling and cohesive online presence.

Adding a compelling featured image to your post is like choosing the perfect cover for a book. It's your chance to pique the curiosity of your audience, to create an emotional connection, and to convey the core message or theme of your content. It's the visual representation of your storytelling, setting the tone for what's to come and providing an immediate visual context.

Visual appeal is an integral part of effective content, and a captivating featured image can significantly enhance the overall aesthetics and engagement of your posts. Readers are naturally drawn to images, and a well-chosen featured image can break up text, provide visual interest, and guide readers through the content. It's a vital element in the art of storytelling, making your content more inviting and accessible.

Moreover, in the age of social media and content sharing, the featured image often serves as the face of your content when shared on platforms like Facebook, Twitter, or LinkedIn. It can mean the difference between a potential reader scrolling past your content or clicking to learn more. A compelling featured image can be the digital billboard that stops the scrolling thumb and captures the viewer's attention.

Excerpt

The excerpt, in the context of WordPress and content management, plays a crucial role in engaging and captivating your audience. It serves as a concise summary or a sneak peek of what readers can expect when they click to access the full post. In essence, the excerpt is your opportunity to provide a compelling teaser, a literary appetizer, if you will, that invites readers to delve deeper into the heart of your content.

By default, WordPress offers a helpful feature where it generates an excerpt automatically based on the post's content. This automated process extracts the initial portion of your post, usually the first few sentences or paragraphs, to create the excerpt. However, it's important to note that this automated method might not always encapsulate the essence of your post effectively, especially if you have a longer article with diverse themes.

Here's where the beauty of customization comes into play. WordPress allows you the creative freedom to craft a custom excerpt tailored to your precise needs. This custom excerpt can be carefully composed to encapsulate the core message, themes, or even an intriguing hook from your post. In essence, it empowers you to take charge of the narrative you want to convey to your audience.

Discussion

The discussion settings in WordPress allow you to control whether comments are enabled or disabled for a particular post or page. Comments provide an avenue for visitor interaction, allowing them to share their thoughts, ask questions, and engage in discussions related to your content. You can choose to enable or disable comments globally or on a per-post/page basis.

Understanding these elements related to posts and pages in WordPress will help you create well-structured, engaging content that resonates with your audience. By utilizing features like visibility options, publishing settings, categories, tags, featured images, excerpts, and discussion controls, you can enhance the user experience and drive meaningful interactions on your website.

Remember, the key to successful content creation lies in finding the right balance between informative, visually appealing, and user-friendly elements. With WordPress's versatile platform, you have the tools at your disposal to create compelling posts and pages that captivate and inspire your readers.

(10) WordPress Settings

Now we will explore the various settings available in WordPress that allow you to customize and fine-tune your website. These settings cover different aspects of your site's functionality and appearance. Let's delve into the key settings sections. Settings link is located on the left-hand side.

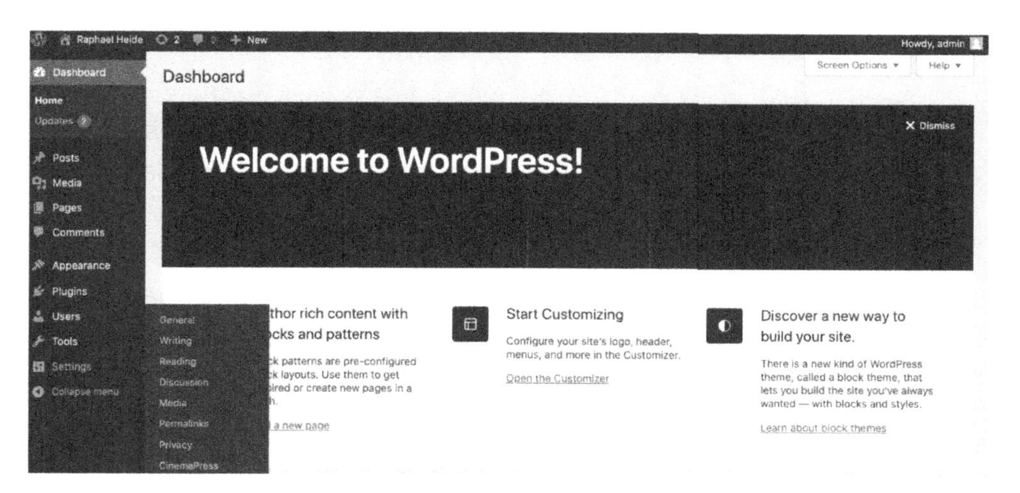

General Settings

The General settings section contains fundamental configuration options for your WordPress site. Here are the key settings you'll encounter:

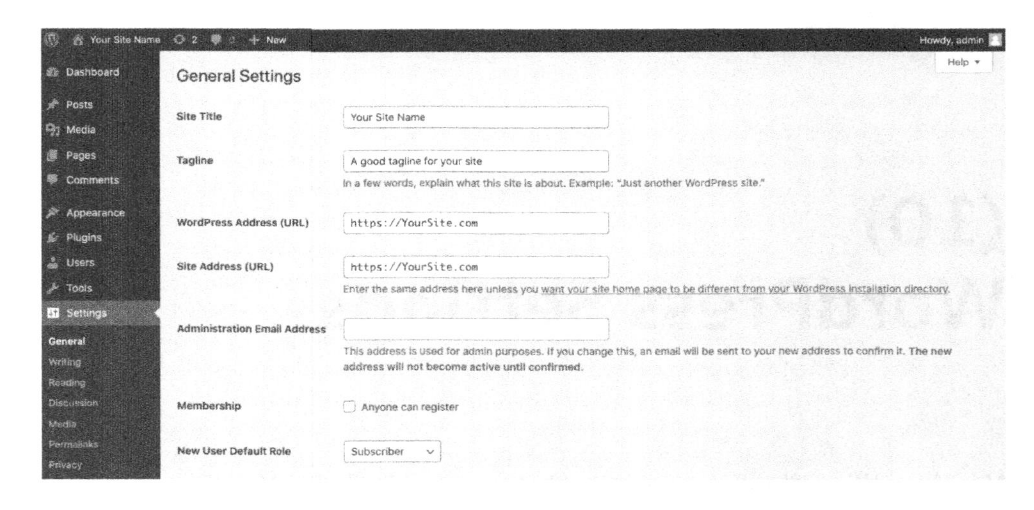

At the end of this book, you will find supporting materials, such as links to high-resolution images and much more.

Site Title: This is the name of your website or blog. It is typically displayed in the browser's title bar and used as the default heading for your site.

Tagline: The tagline provides a brief description or slogan for your site. It helps visitors understand the purpose or focus of your website. It is typically displayed alongside your site title or logo in the header area. The tagline helps visitors understand what your website is about and can be a memorable phrase that captures the essence of your brand or the content you provide. It is an important element for branding and making a strong first impression on your audience.

WordPress Address (URL) and Site Address (URL): These

settings define the web addresses (URLs) for your WordPress site. Ensure they accurately reflect your domain name and site structure.

Timezone: Select your desired timezone to ensure accurate time display for scheduled posts, comments, and other time-related functions.

Date and Time Format: Customize how dates and times are displayed on your site.

Choose the desired format from the available options or enter a custom format using the provided placeholders. The placeholders represent different components of the date and time, such as day, month, year, hour, minute, and second.

Out of the box, WordPress offers a selection of pre-defined date and time format options, each catering to different preferences and locales. These formats, automatically rendered when you display dates and times on your website, include:

"F j, Y" - Example: January 1, 2024

"m/d/Y" - Example: 01/01/2024

"h:i A" - Example: 12:00 PM

"j F Y" - Example: 1 January 2024

"M jS, Y" - Example: Jan 1st, 2024

These predefined formats are particularly useful for those who don't wish to delve into the intricacies of customizing their date and time presentations.

However, WordPress doesn't stop there. It empowers users to wield a degree of creative control over how temporal information is showcased on their websites. This is achieved through the use of custom date and time formats, which allow you to craft your own unique presentations.

At the core of these custom formats are placeholders representing different temporal elements. These placeholders are placeholders like:

"Y" for the year (e.g., 2024)

"F" for the full month name (e.g., January)

"j" for the day of the month (e.g., 1)

"g" for the hour without leading zeros (e.g., 1)

"i" for the minutes (e.g., 00)

"A" for uppercase AM or PM (e.g., PM)

By combining these placeholders, you can concoct your very own format. For example, if you desire a format like "Y/m/j g:i A," WordPress will yield a presentation like "2024/01/1 1:00 PM."

The beauty of WordPress's date and time formatting capabilities is further elevated by its ability to incorporate custom text and separators. For instance, if you'd like to include a textual descriptor, you can append it to your format. If you want to use a dash or a comma as a separator, simply include it within your custom format.

Consider the example of creating a format like "l, F jS, Y - g:i

A" which yields a presentation such as "Monday, January 1st, 2024 - 1:00 PM." In this format, "l" represents the full weekday name, and the dash is used as a separator before the time.

Enhancing User Experience

Why does all this matter? Tailoring your date and time formats is more than just aesthetics; it's about enhancing the user experience. Your audience, whether they're readers, customers, or community members, interacts with your website's content, and how you present temporal information can impact their perception and understanding.

By choosing or crafting the right format, you can align your date and time presentations with your website's tone, purpose, and target audience. Whether it's a news site delivering up-to-the-minute information, a personal blog sharing life's moments, or an e-commerce platform displaying product availability, WordPress's flexibility in date and time formatting ensures that time remains a valuable part of your narrative.

Membership: Choose whether you want to allow anyone to register as a user on your site or limit registration to specific roles. We will talk about Membership in Users on this book.

Site Language: Select the language used for your site's backend administration interface.

WordPress understands that the internet is a global village, and it caters to this diversity by offering its platform in over 100 different languages. This is an impressive feat, given the myriad cultures, languages, and regions that make up the online landscape. Whether you're a blogger, an e-commerce entrepreneur, a nonprofit organization, or a corporation, WordPress ensures that you have the tools to communicate effectively with your target audience, irrespective of their location or linguistic preferences.

This multilingual and multiregional prowess is achieved through a process known as localization and internationalization. Localization is the adaptation of software for a specific region or language. WordPress translation teams, comprising dedicated volunteers, work tirelessly to ensure that the platform's core elements and user interface are presented in a manner that resonates with users from different linguistic backgrounds. It's the reason you can navigate your WordPress site in not only English but also Spanish, French, Japanese, Arabic, and countless other languages.

Internationalization, on the other hand, is the process of making software flexible enough to be adapted to multiple languages and regions. WordPress employs internationalization techniques that allow themes, plugins, and the core software to be customized or extended to support a wide array of linguistic and regional preferences.

When you embark on your WordPress journey, one of the initial choices you make is selecting your preferred language and region. This setting determines the language of your WordPress dashboard, making it comfortable and accessible for you to work with. It's also the language in which you'll receive important notifications and updates.

Furthermore, the language and region setting can extend to your site's content. You have the ability to create content in multiple languages or variations of a single language to cater to diverse audiences. This feature is particularly beneficial if your website has a global reach and you want to offer content in, say, English (USA) and English (UK), tailoring the language to specific regional nuances and spellings.

WordPress's commitment to language diversity is not just about interface translation. It's about ensuring that the internet remains an inclusive space, where people can access, share, and interact with content in their preferred languages. This commitment is instrumental in expanding the reach and impact of digital content, facilitating cross-border communication, and fostering a sense of belonging for users around the world.

Writing Settings

The Writing settings section allows you to configure default settings related to content creation and publishing. Here are the main options you'll encounter:

Default Post Category: The default post category in WordPress refers to the category that is automatically assigned to a blog post when no specific category is selected. It acts as a fallback option for posts that don't have a specific category assigned to them.

By default, WordPress assigns the "Uncategorized" category as the default post category. However, you have the flexibility to change this default category to a different one or create new categories to better suit your website's content organization. We will talk about Categories on this book.

Default Post Format: Choose the default format for your posts, such as standard, aside, gallery, or video. This option is theme-dependent and may not be available in all themes.

Default Post Editor: Select the editor you prefer for creating and editing posts. WordPress offers two options: the Classic Editor and the newer Gutenberg Block Editor.

Check Gutenberg Chapter to know more about Gutenberg.

Before the Gutenberg editor was introduced in WordPress version 5.0, the Classic Editor was the default editing interface in WordPress. It featured a single content field where users could enter their text and media, and it relied on the use of plugins and custom code to extend its functionality.

Update Services: WordPress automatically notifies various update services when you publish or update a post. You can add or remove services from the default list.

Reading Settings

The Reading settings section allows you to control how your site's content is displayed to visitors. Here are the important settings you'll find:

Your homepage displays: Choose whether you want your homepage to display your latest posts or a static page. If you choose a static page, you can select separate pages for your homepage and blog posts.

Blog pages show at most: Set the number of posts you want to display on each page of your blog.

Syndication feeds show the most recent: Syndication feeds that show the most recent content refer to a feature in WordPress that allows users to subscribe to a feed and receive updates whenever new content is published on a website. These feeds are commonly known as RSS (Really Simple Syndication) or Atom feeds.

When you enable syndication feeds in WordPress, you provide a way for users to stay updated with your website's latest posts, news, or any other published content. The syndication feed will automatically deliver the most recent content to subscribers' feed readers or email clients, allowing them to conveniently access and read your latest updates without having to visit your website directly.

The "most recent" aspect of syndication feeds means that the feed will display the latest content in chronological order, with the newest posts appearing at the top. Subscribers will see the most recently published articles or updates first when they access the feed.

WordPress provides built-in support for syndication feeds, and the feed functionality is typically enabled by default. Users can subscribe to your feed by clicking on the feed icon (usually represented by the orange RSS logo) or by entering the feed URL into their preferred feed reader.

Syndication feeds are a powerful tool for content distribution and keeping your audience informed about your latest content. They provide a convenient way for users to stay up to date with your website without actively visiting it.

Search Engine Visibility: If you don't want search engines to index your site, you can discourage search engines from indexing it. However, keep in mind that this option is not foolproof and doesn't guarantee privacy.

Discussion Settings

The Discussion settings control how comments are managed on your WordPress site. Here are the important options you'll encounter:

> **Default article settings:** Choose whether you want to allow comments on new articles, enable pingbacks and trackbacks, and whether you want to display the comments in reverse order (newest at the top).
>
>> **Pingbacks:** Pingbacks are a form of automated notifications that WordPress generates when another website links to your site. When a website with pingbacks enabled links to one of your posts, WordPress automatically sends a pingback to your site. This pingback appears as a comment on the post that was linked to, indicating that another website has referenced your content.
>>
>> **Trackbacks:** Trackbacks are similar to pingbacks but require manual approval. When another website links to your post and has trackbacks enabled, it sends a trackback request to your site. The trackback appears as a comment in the moderation queue of your WordPress admin panel. You have the option to approve or deny the trackback.

Both pingbacks and trackbacks provide a way for websites to communicate with each other, creating a network of interlinked content. They help to promote discussions and collaborations across different sites.

It's important to note that pingbacks and trackbacks can be subject to spam, as spammers may attempt to abuse these features. WordPress provides moderation tools to help you manage and filter these notifications effectively, ensuring that legitimate pingbacks and trackbacks are approved while spam is blocked.

In newer versions of WordPress, pingbacks and trackbacks are often disabled by default due to their susceptibility to spam. However, you can enable them manually in the discussion settings of your WordPress admin panel if you wish to receive these notifications and engage with other websites through pingbacks and trackbacks.

Other comment settings: Configure settings related to comment moderation, such as requiring manual approval for comments, enabling comment author must fill out name and email, and setting a maximum number of links allowed in comments.

Email notifications: Determine whether you want to receive email notifications for various comment-related events, such as when a comment is held for moderation or when a comment is posted.

Media Settings

The Media settings section allows you to control how media files (such as images, videos, and audio) are handled and displayed on your site. Here are the key settings you'll find:

Thumbnail size: Define the default size for thumbnail images generated by WordPress. This size is used for displaying thumbnails in various areas of your site.

We will see later:

In the context of WordPress, a thumbnail refers to a

small, scaled-down version of an image that is used to represent or preview a larger image or post content.

Thumbnails play a significant role in enhancing the visual appeal and user experience of a WordPress website. They are commonly used in various areas, including blog post listings, galleries, sliders, and featured image sections.

When creating or editing a post or page in WordPress, you have the option to set a featured image. This featured image is often displayed as a thumbnail alongside the post title or excerpt on your website's homepage, archive pages, or wherever the post is listed. The thumbnail helps to provide a visual representation of the content, enticing users to click and read more.

Medium size and Large size: Specify the dimensions for medium-sized and large-sized images.

Uploading files: Choose whether you want to organize uploaded files into month- and year-based folders for easier management. The file will be organized inside your web hosting.

Permalinks Settings

Permalinks determine the structure of your website's URLs. It is important to choose a permalink structure that is both user-friendly and search engine optimized. Here are the common permalink options you'll encounter:

Plain: This option uses the default WordPress URL structure, which includes parameters and question marks. It is not recommended for SEO purposes or for creating readable URLs.

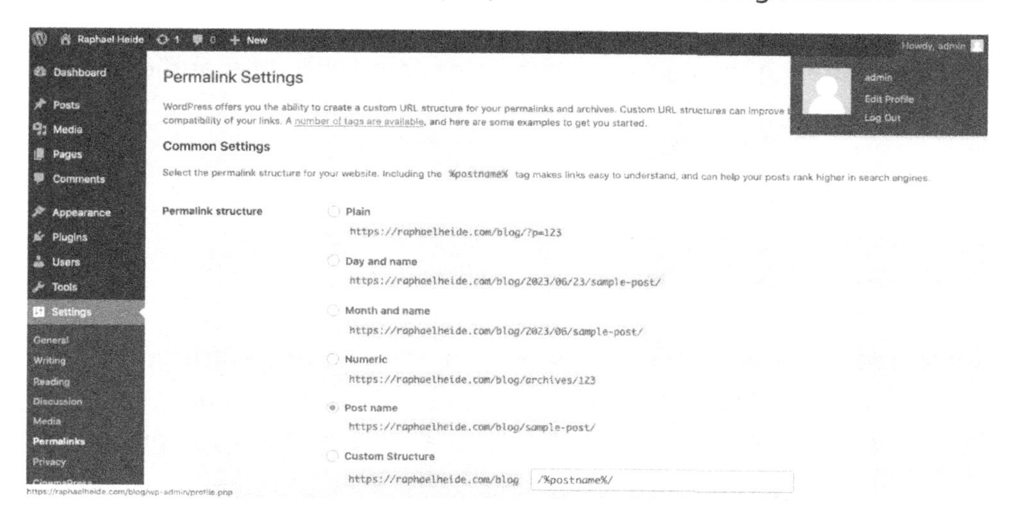

Day and name, Month and name, Numeric, Post name: These options use different combinations of date and post name elements to create the URL structure.

Custom Structure: This option allows you to define a custom permalink structure using placeholders such as %postname% (post name) or %category% (category name) - It's the best option for SEO (you can check Chapter SEO).

Privacy Settings

The Privacy settings section helps you configure the privacy policy for your WordPress site. You can specify whether you want to display a privacy policy page and set the page that should be used. This is important for compliance with data protection regulations.

It's crucial to review and adjust these settings according to your website's requirements and your preferences. By properly configuring the discussion settings, managing media settings, optimizing permalink structure, and addressing privacy concerns, you can enhance the user experience, engage with your audience, and ensure your website adheres to privacy regulations.

Remember to Save

Remember to save your changes after modifying any settings. Regularly reviewing and updating these settings will ensure that your WordPress site remains optimized, secure, and in line with your goals and audience needs.

In the next chapter, we will explore advanced settings and features in WordPress, including user management, plugins, themes, and more, empowering you to unlock the full potential of your website.

(11) WordPress Users

We'll embark on a journey through the intricacies of user management in WordPress. In the world of website administration, users are the lifeblood, and knowing how to manage them effectively is paramount for maintaining a secure, organized, and thriving online presence.

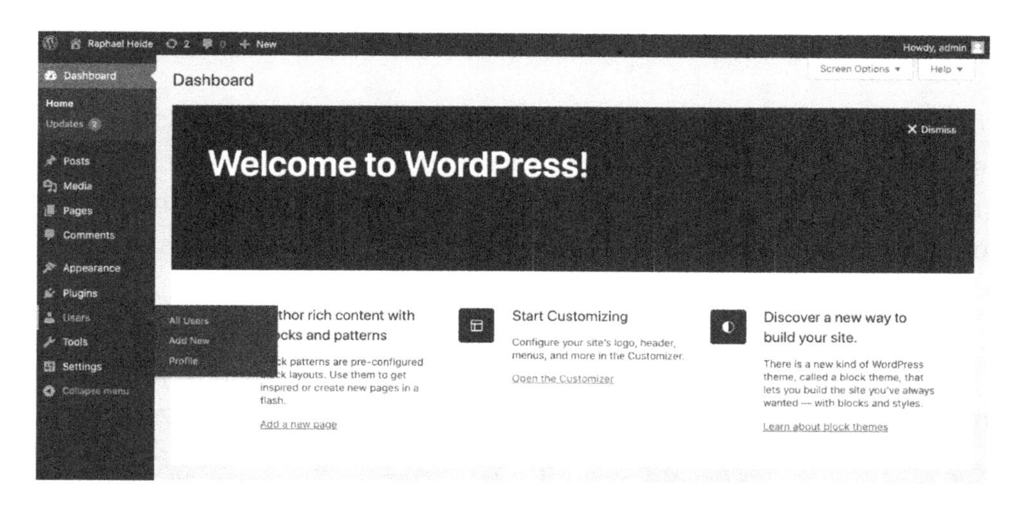

We'll navigate through essential aspects, including the "All Users" section, the process of adding new users, and the nuances of managing user profiles. To kick things off, you can find the **Users**

link conveniently located on the left-hand side of your WordPress dashboard.

So, without further ado, let's dive into the realm of WordPress user management and empower you with the knowledge and skills to maintain a harmonious and secure online community.

All Users

The "All Users" section is your central hub for managing all registered users on your WordPress site. Here, you can view key user details such as usernames, roles, email addresses, and registration dates. Additionally, you have the ability to edit user profiles, delete users, and assign different roles.

Add New User

To add a new user to your WordPress site, navigate to the "Add New" section. Here, you can create user accounts by filling out the required information, including username, email address, password, and user role. User roles define the level of access and capabilities a user has within the WordPress system. Common user roles include:

For Your Information

Administrator (full access and can access the admin panel).

Editor (can use some place of admin panel and edit posts and pages).

Author (can create posts and pages and delete own posts and pages).

Contributor (can work send some texts to author).

Subscriber (just can subscriber on website).

Select the appropriate role based on the user's responsibilities and permissions needed. You need to make the right decision when define a role for an user. In this chapter I will talk more about each role.

User Profiles

Each user in WordPress has a profile that contains personal information and settings. To access and manage user profiles, click on the user's name in the "All Users" section or select "Your Profile" under the "Users" menu. Within the user profile, you can:

Update personal information: Modify the user's display name, email address, and other contact details.

Change password: Reset the user's password or generate a new one.

User bio and avatar: Add a brief biography and choose an avatar or profile picture.

An avatar, in the context of online platforms and websites, refers to a graphical representation or image that represents a person or user. It is a visual representation of an individual, typically displayed alongside their username or profile information.

Avatars can take various forms, such as a photograph, a cartoonish image, an icon, or any other graphical representation chosen by the user. They serve as a means of personalization and identification, allowing users to visually represent themselves in online communities, social networks, forums, and other interactive platforms.

Admin color scheme: Select a color scheme for the user's admin interface.

Additional contact information: Provide additional contact details, such as social media profiles or website URLs.

User role and capabilities: Review and adjust the user's role and capabilities if necessary.

Managing user profiles allows you to ensure accurate information and tailor settings for each user. This can be particularly useful for multi-author websites or when granting specific permissions to contributors or editors.

Remember, it is important to regularly review your user list, remove any unused accounts, and update user permissions as needed to maintain a secure and efficient WordPress environment.

User roles and capabilities in WordPress determine the level of access and permissions granted to different users on a website. Understanding user roles is essential for effectively managing user accounts and controlling what each user can do within the WordPress system. Here are the common user roles in WordPress and their associated capabilities.

Let's remember:

Administrator: The Administrator role has the highest level of access and control over the entire WordPress website.

Administrators can perform tasks such as managing plugins and themes, creating and editing posts/pages, managing other user accounts, changing site settings, and more.

Editor: Editors have the ability to manage and publish content on the website. They can create, edit, publish, and delete their own posts, as well as moderate comments on those posts. However, they cannot perform administrative tasks like installing plugins or changing site settings.

Author: Authors have the capability to create and manage their own posts. They can publish, edit, and delete their own content but cannot modify or publish content created by other users.

Contributor: Contributors can write and manage their own posts, but they need approval from an Editor or Administrator to publish their content. They do not have access to other users' posts and cannot modify or publish content from other contributors.

Subscriber: Subscribers have the most limited role and are usually used for user registration and membership purposes. They can only manage their own user profile and leave comments on posts.

(12)
WordPress Tools

Now we will explore the tools available in WordPress that assist in managing and maintaining your website. These tools provide functionalities such as importing and exporting content, ensuring site health, and handling personal data. Tools link is located on the left-hand side. Let's delve into the tools at your disposal!

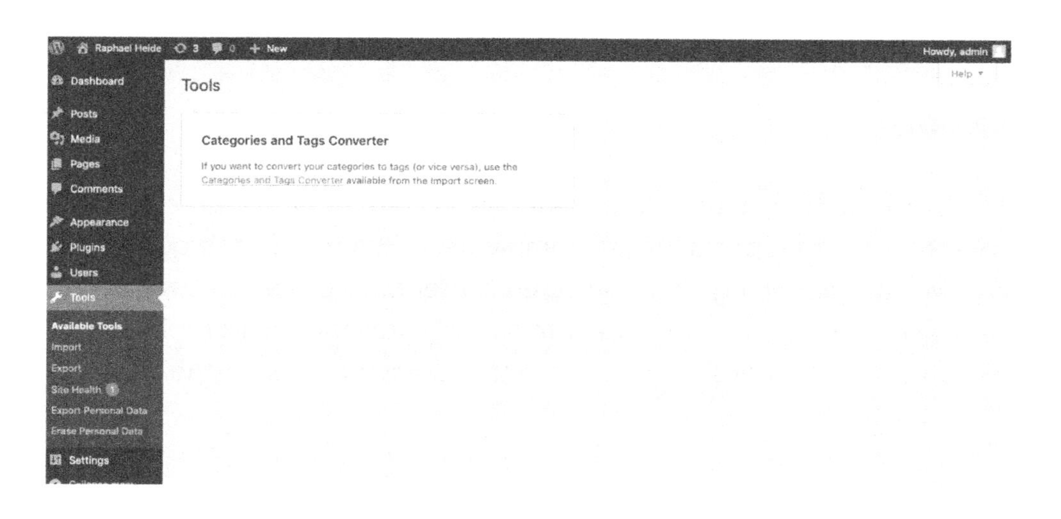

Available Tools

WordPress offers a range of built-in tools that can enhance your website management experience. These tools can be found under the "Tools" menu in your WordPress admin dashboard. The specific tools available may vary depending on your WordPress version and installed plugins.

Import

The Import tool allows you to import content from other platforms or WordPress installations. This is particularly useful when migrating your website from one host to another or when consolidating content from multiple sources. WordPress provides options to import content from various platforms, including Blogger, Tumblr, and other WordPress installations.

Export

The Export tool enables you to create backups of your WordPress content, including posts, pages, comments, and other data. It generates an XML file containing all the selected content, which can be used to restore your website or migrate it to a new installation. This tool is valuable for safeguarding your content and ensuring its portability.

Site Health

The Site Health tool helps you monitor and optimize the performance and security of your WordPress site. It provides insights into the overall health of your website and offers recommendations to improve its functionality and security. Site Health checks your WordPress installation for potential issues, outdated software, and provides suggestions to optimize performance and enhance security.

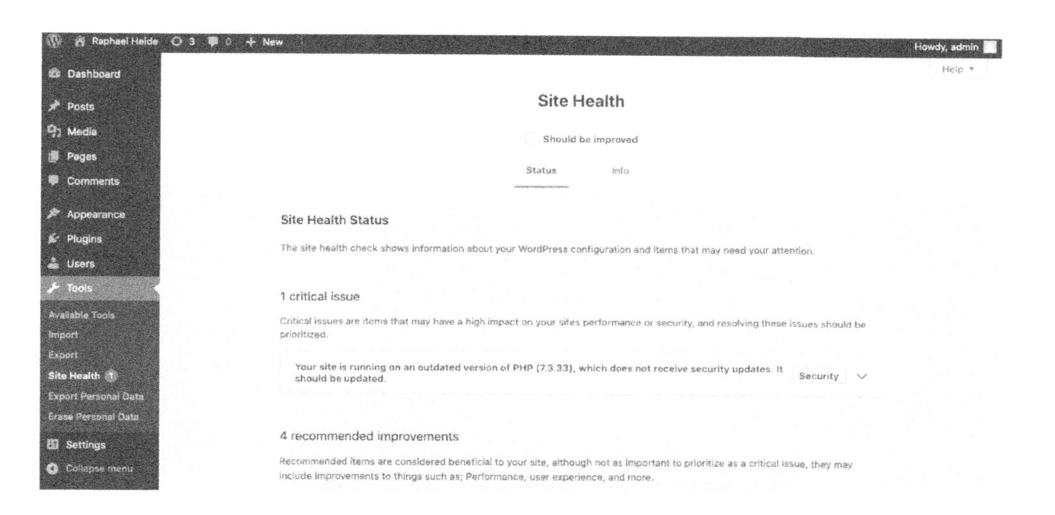

Export Personal Data

WordPress is committed to user privacy and data protection. The Export Personal Data tool allows you to generate a file containing the personal data associated with a particular user account. This feature is particularly relevant if you need to comply with data protection regulations or fulfill data access requests from users.

Erase Personal Data

In accordance with data protection regulations, WordPress includes the Erase Personal Data tool. This tool enables you to remove all personal data associated with a specific user account. It helps ensure compliance with data privacy requirements and gives users control over their personal information.

Utilizing these WordPress tools empowers you to manage and optimize your website effectively. Whether you need to import content, export backups, monitor site health, handle personal data export, or erase personal data, these tools simplify crucial tasks and enhance your website management experience.

(13) WordPress Plugins

We'll embark on a journey into the dynamic universe of WordPress plugins. In the world of website management, plugins are the versatile and indispensable tools that empower you to supercharge your WordPress website with additional features and functionalities.

We'll delve into the very essence of what plugins are, why they hold such importance in the WordPress ecosystem, and how to efficiently manage them. Throughout this chapter, we'll cover a wide array of plugin-related tasks, equipping you with the knowledge and skills to enhance your website in a way that aligns perfectly with your unique goals and requirements.

To kickstart this enlightening journey, you can find the Plugins link conveniently located on the left-hand side of your WordPress dashboard. So, without further ado, let's dive headfirst into the realm of WordPress plugins and unlock the true potential of your website. Let's get started.

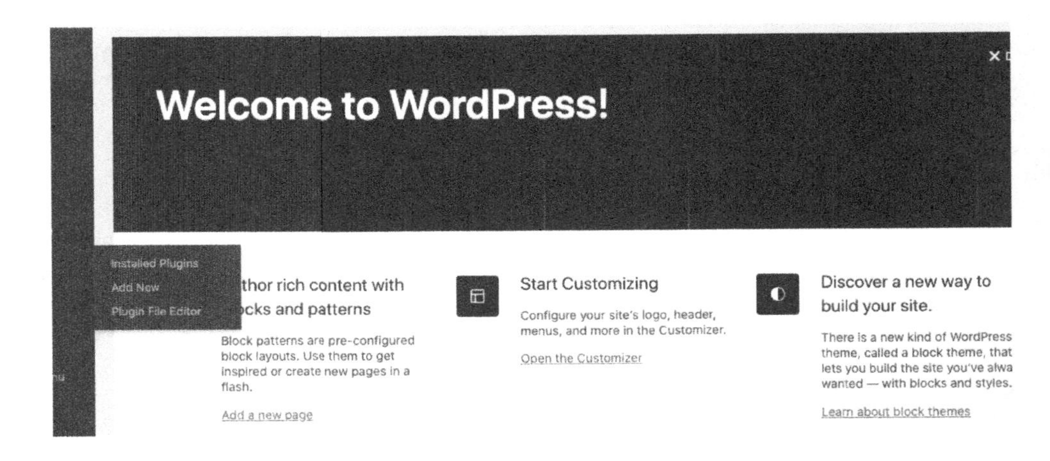

What is a Plugin?

A plugin is a piece of software that extends the capabilities of your WordPress website. It adds new features, functionality, or modifies existing elements of your site. Plugins are designed to be easily installable and customizable, allowing you to tailor your website to meet specific needs without requiring coding skills.

Why Plugins are Important

Plugins play a vital role in extending the functionality of your WordPress site. They allow you to add features such as contact forms, social media integration, search engine optimization, security enhancements, e-commerce capabilities, and much more. Plugins provide flexibility and customization options to make your website unique and meet your specific requirements.

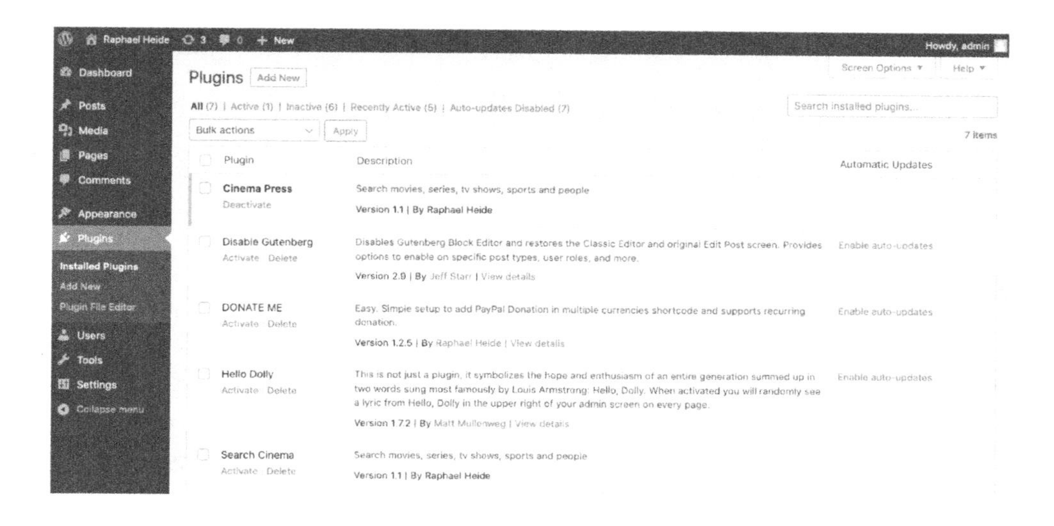

Installed Plugins

The "Installed Plugins" section in your WordPress admin dashboard displays all the plugins currently installed on your website. Here, you can view information about each plugin, such as its name, description, version, and status (active or inactive). You can also activate, deactivate, update, or delete plugins directly from this section.

For Your Information

Once you are on the "Installed Plugins" page, you will see a list of all the plugins installed on your website. The active plugins will be marked with a status of "Active" below their respective names.

You can easily identify if a plugin is active by checking its status in the list. If a plugin is inactive, it will be marked as "Inactive." Additionally, active plugins may have additional settings or options available, depending on their functionality.

By reviewing the list of installed plugins and their status, you can determine which plugins are currently active on your WordPress website.

Add New Plugin

To add new plugins to your WordPress site, navigate to the "Add New" section under the "Plugins" menu. Here, you can search for plugins from the WordPress plugin repository, upload plugins from your computer, or install plugins from external sources. Once installed, you can activate and configure the plugins to suit your needs.

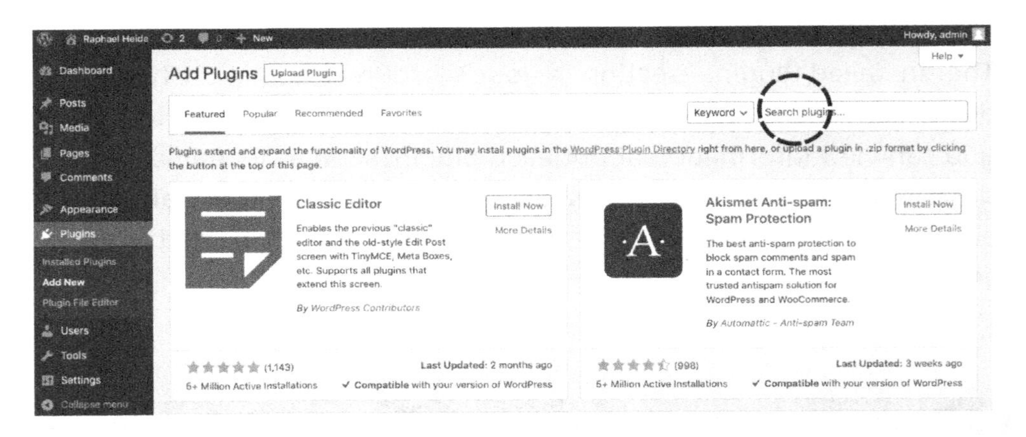

You can search plugins directly from your WordPress panel. After find your plugin you can install and active the plugin.

If you have a plugin in your computer, you can upload a new plugin. You can also search a plugin in the WordPress Plugin Directory: https://wordpress.org/plugins/

To upload a plugin to your WordPress website from your computer, you can follow these steps:

Download the Plugin: Visit the official WordPress Plugin Directory or any reputable plugin marketplace to find the desired plugin. Download the plugin file to your computer. The file will typically be in a ZIP format.

Log in to Your WordPress Admin Panel: Open your web browser and navigate to the login page of your WordPress website. Enter your username and password to log in to the admin panel.

Go to the Plugins Page: Once logged in, click on "Plugins" in the left sidebar of the admin panel. This will take you to the Plugins page, where you can manage your installed plugins.

Click on "Add New": On the Plugins page, click on the "Add New" button at the top. This will take you to the Add Plugins page.

Upload the Plugin: On the Add Plugins page, click on the "Upload Plugin" button at the top. This will reveal a plugin upload form.

Choose the Plugin File: Click on the "Choose File" button, which will open a file selection dialog on your computer. Locate and select the plugin file you downloaded in Step 1.

Install the Plugin: Once you have selected the plugin file, click on the "Install Now" button. WordPress will upload and install the plugin from the file you provided.

Activate the Plugin: After the plugin is successfully installed, you will see a confirmation message. Click on the "Activate Plugin" link to activate the plugin on your website.

Configure the Plugin: Depending on the plugin, you may need to configure its settings. Some plugins have a dedicated settings page under the "Settings" menu, while others may provide configuration options directly on the Plugins page or in their own separate menu.

Once the plugin is activated and configured, you can start using its features and functionality on your WordPress website.

For Your Information

It's important to download plugins from trusted sources to ensure their security and compatibility with your WordPress version. Additionally, make sure to keep your plugins updated to benefit from bug fixes, new features, and security patches.

You can check the book "101 WordPress Plugins... and Then Some". I talk about the best and popular plugins.

Plugin File Editor

WordPress provides a built-in Plugin File Editor that allows you to modify the code of your installed plugins. However, it is important to exercise caution when using this feature, as any incorrect changes can break your website or cause conflicts. It is recommended to have a backup and some coding knowledge before making modifications using the Plugin File Editor.

How to Update a Plugin

WordPress regularly releases updates for plugins to improve functionality, fix bugs, and ensure compatibility with the latest WordPress version. To update a plugin, go to the "Installed Plugins" section, and if an update is available, you will see a notification. Simply click the "Update Now" link to update the plugin to its latest version.

How to Delete a Plugin

If you no longer need a plugin or want to remove it from your website, you can delete it. In the "Installed Plugins" section, find the plugin you wish to remove and click the "Delete" link below it. WordPress will prompt you to confirm the deletion. Be cautious when deleting plugins, as it may remove associated data or functionality from your site.

WordPress plugins offer endless possibilities to enhance and customize your website. Whether it's improving functionality, adding new features, or optimizing your site's performance, plugins provide a powerful way to extend the capabilities of your WordPress site.

(14) Appearance

Now we will explore the "Appearance" section of your WordPress admin dashboard. This section allows you to manage the visual aspects of your website, including themes, widgets, menus, backgrounds, and more. Appearance is located on the left-hand side. Let's dive in and discover the various options available to customize your website's appearance.

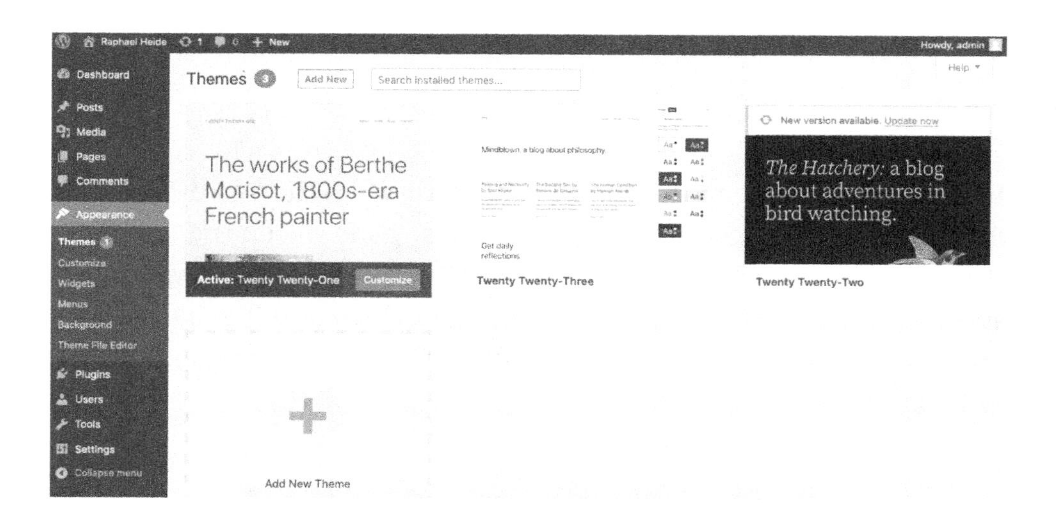

Themes

Themes play a crucial role in determining the overall look and feel of your WordPress website. They control the layout, color schemes, typography, and other visual elements. In the "Appearance" section, you can access and manage your installed themes.

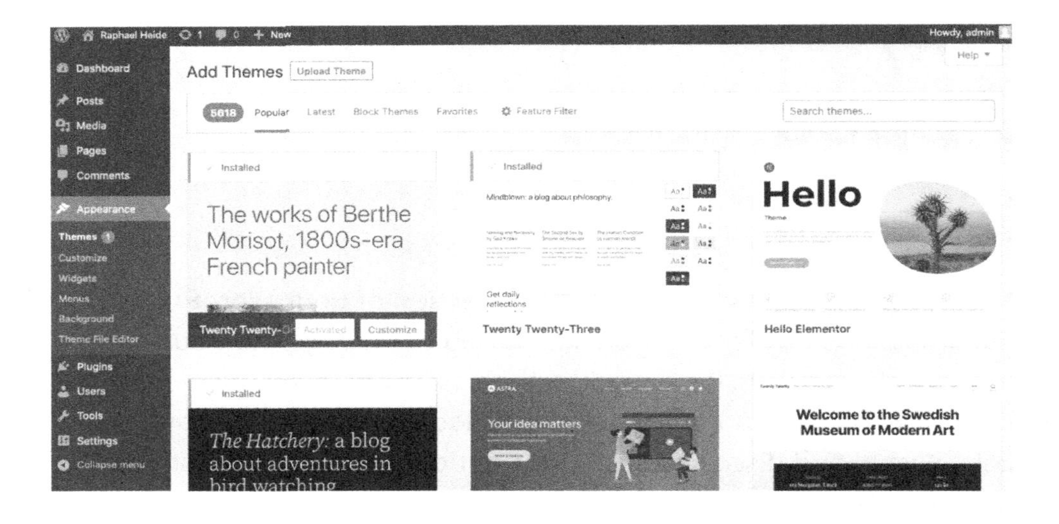

Add a New Theme Online

To add a new theme to your website directly from the WordPress theme repository, navigate to the "Themes" page within the "Appearance" section. Click on the "Add New" button to browse and search for a wide range of free themes. Once you find a theme you like, click the "Install" button, and WordPress will handle the installation process.

Add a New Theme from Your Computer

If you have a premium or custom theme that you've obtained from a third-party source, you can upload it to your WordPress website. In the "Themes" page, click on the "Upload Theme" button. Choose the theme file from your computer and click "Install Now" to upload and install the theme.

Activate a Theme

Once you have added a new theme to your website, you need to activate it to make it visible to your visitors. On the "Themes" page, find the theme you want to activate and click the "Activate" button. Your website will now use the selected theme's design and layout.

Customize a Theme

WordPress 6.1 and below: WordPress provides a built-in theme customizer that allows you to modify various aspects of your active theme. Access the "Customize" option under the "Appearance" section to make changes to colors, fonts, header, footer, and other theme-specific settings. The live preview feature enables you to see the changes in real-time before applying them. It's really simple: you just need make your changes and save.

Check the steps: s

> **Access the Theme Customizer:** In your WordPress admin panel, go to "Appearance" and click on "Customize." This will open the Theme Customizer, where you can make changes to your theme.

Explore the options: The Theme Customizer provides various sections and options to customize your theme. These may include options for site identity (logo, site title, tagline), colors, fonts, header, footer, menus, widgets, and more.

Make changes: Click on each section or option to expand and reveal the available settings. Modify the settings according to your preferences. For example, you can change colors, upload a custom logo, adjust font styles, rearrange widgets, or set a custom background image.

Preview and save changes: As you make changes, the live preview of your website will update in real-time. Take advantage of the preview to see how your modifications affect the appearance. If you are satisfied with the changes, click the "Save & Publish" button to apply them to your site.

Additional customization options: Depending on the theme you're using, you may have additional customization options. Some themes provide their own customization panels or settings pages, offering more advanced options for layout, page templates, post formats, and more. Explore these options to further tailor your theme.

Remember to save your changes regularly and check how they affect your website on different devices and screen sizes to ensure a consistent and responsive design.

It's worth noting that more advanced customization may require knowledge of HTML, CSS, and possibly PHP. If you're comfortable with coding, you can further customize your theme by modifying template files or using custom CSS code.

Overall, WordPress offers a user-friendly customization experience through the Theme Customizer, allowing you to personalize your website's look and feel without extensive coding knowledge.

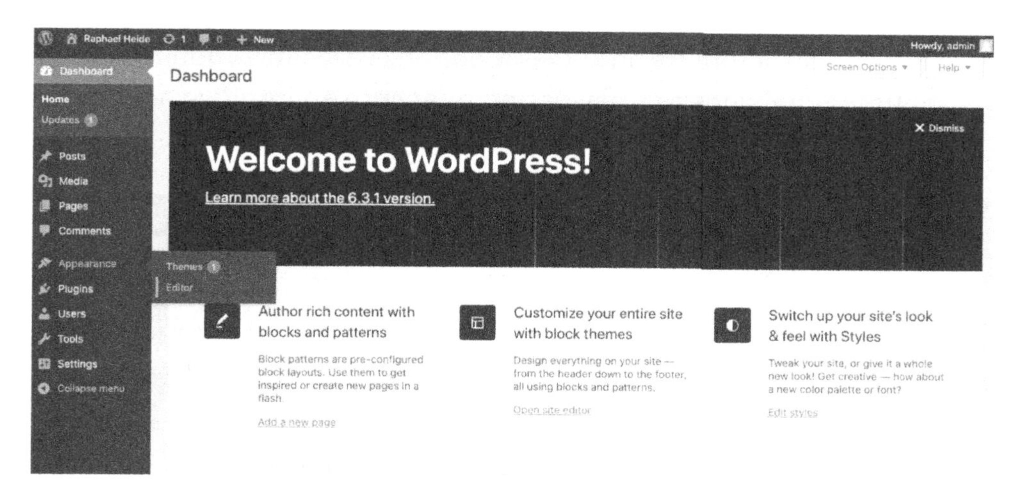

WordPress 6.2 and up: You have a new customize link, called Editor. You can find in your left-side menu "Appearance -> Editor." If you want unlock all power of Editor, update your WordPress to 6.3 or 6.4.

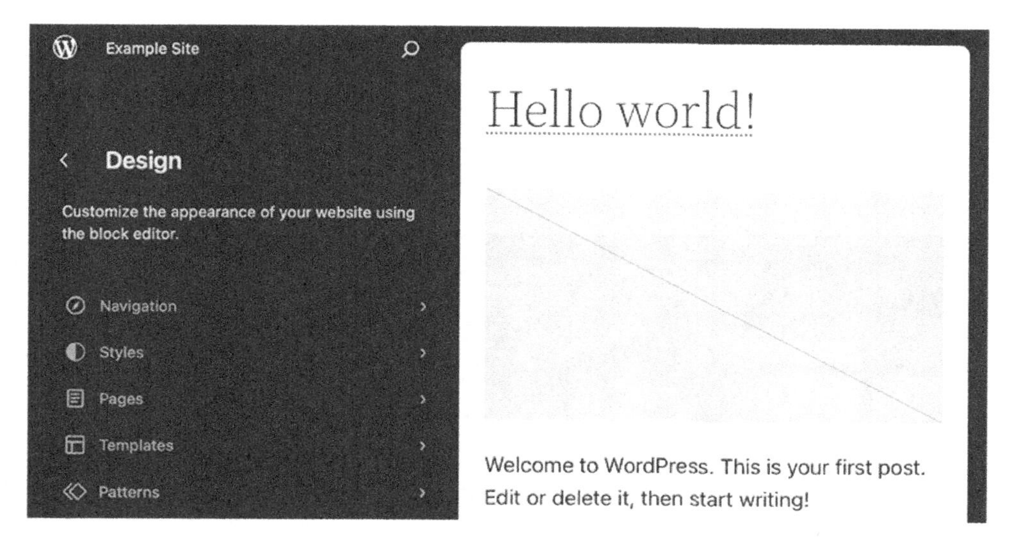

The new WordPress 6.3 has a beautiful and easy panel. It's the place for you design your website.

Navigation: This menu is where you manage the links in your website's navigation block. You have the flexibility to rearrange menu items, delete items, and make changes to the menu structure using the Edit option. This allows you to fine-tune your website's navigation to ensure an intuitive and user-friendly experience.

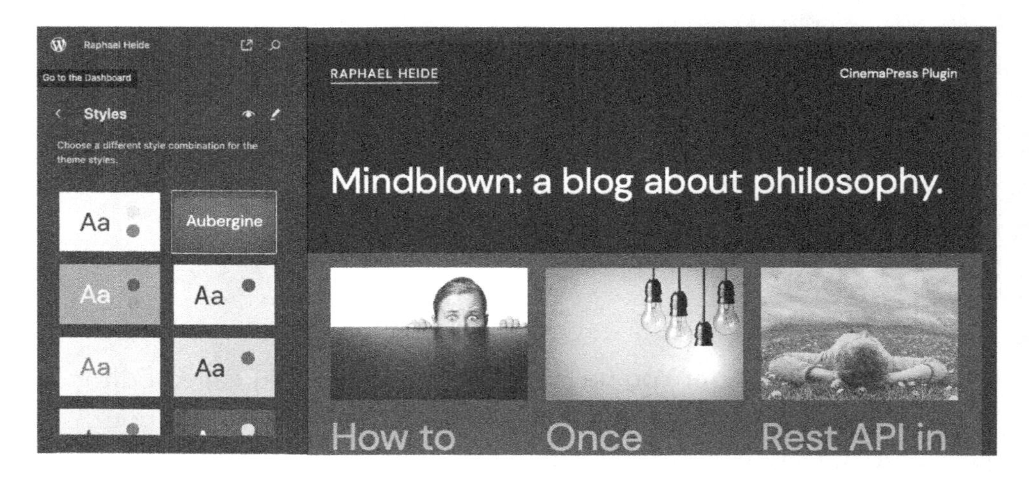

Styles: In the Styles menu, you have the power to select and preview different style variations provided by your chosen theme. This feature enables you to customize the visual aesthetics of your website, aligning it with your brand or desired design. You'll also find buttons for accessing the

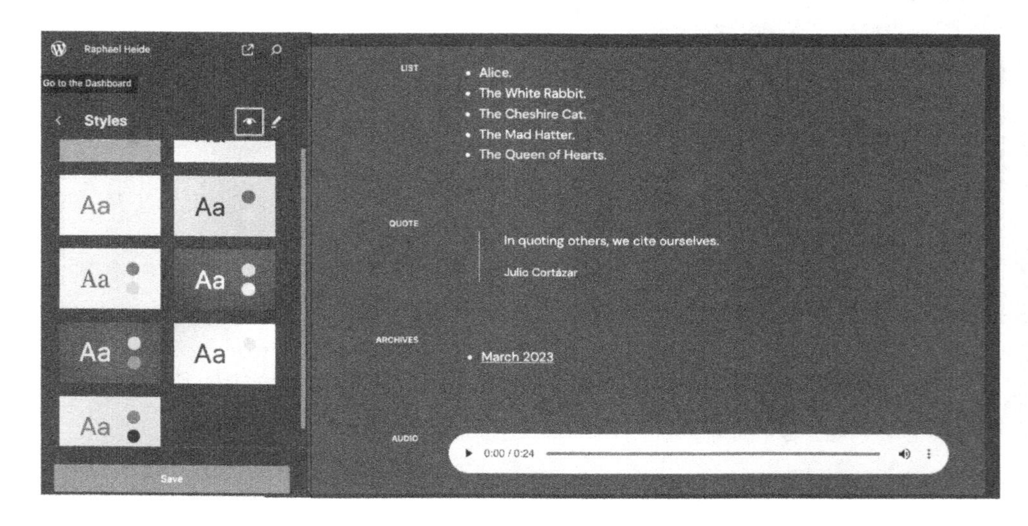

style book and the global styles panel, providing you with comprehensive control over your website's appearance.

If you click on EYE ICON you can see all styles book for each specific style:

Pages: The Pages menu serves as a centralized hub for all the pages available on your website, including drafts. From this menu, you can effortlessly open, edit, and configure your pages directly within the site editor. This streamlined approach simplifies the process of content management and ensures that your pages are up to date and engaging for your visitors.

Templates: This menu offers an array of available templates for your website. You can select a template for editing, similar to the process in the current version. Additionally, you have the creative freedom to create a completely new template, tailored to your specific requirements. This feature empowers you to craft a unique and visually appealing website layout.

Patterns: The Patterns menu is a dynamic addition that replaces the old Template Parts menu. It serves as a repository for both synchronized and unsynchronized patterns, along with template parts. These patterns are design elements or content blocks that you can easily insert into your pages or templates. They offer a convenient way to maintain design consistency and streamline content creation.

Incorporating these menu options into your WordPress workflow allows for a more efficient and customized website-building experience. Whether you're refining navigation, fine-tuning styles, managing pages, creating templates, or utilizing design patterns, these tools provide the versatility and control needed to craft a website that stands out and resonates with your audience.

In WordPress 6.3, we witness two pivotal changes that transform the way we work with reusable blocks, now known as patterns, and the introduction of synced and unsynced options.

First, let's explore the concept of synced patterns. These are reusable blocks that, when modified, automatically update the original pattern. It's a game-changer for efficiency, ensuring that changes made to a synced pattern are consistently reflected throughout your website.

On the other hand, we have unsynced patterns, which function similarly to the traditional block patterns. They offer flexibility, allowing you to make changes without altering the original pattern.

What's truly revolutionary about this update is the accessibility it brings to pattern management. Before WordPress 6.3, creating custom patterns involved a process that didn't directly engage with the Site Editor.

Now, WordPress 6.3 redefines pattern management by providing an intuitive approach within the Site Editor itself. Users can effortlessly view and manage all patterns, making the process of designing and deploying customized patterns remarkably fluid and user-friendly.

This change empowers WordPress users to have more control and creative freedom in designing their websites. With the ability to manage patterns directly from the Site Editor, the process becomes more integrated, efficient, and aligned with the needs of content creators and designers. It's a significant step towards enhancing the user experience and flexibility within the WordPress ecosystem.

Create and Manage Patterns

When you step into the Site Editor within WordPress, the Patterns menu becomes your gateway to a world of creative possibilities. Here, you'll find a wealth of resources to craft your website's design and content.

The Patterns menu provides seamless access to template parts and patterns, giving you the tools to shape your site's visual identity and layout. Whether you're looking to create, save, or manage both synced and unsynced patterns, this menu is your go-to destination.

To kickstart your creative journey, simply locate the enticing "+" icon that beckons you to explore. Clicking on it reveals two distinct choices: "Create template part" and "Create pattern." These options serve as your launchpad for designing, organizing, and optimizing your website's structure and style.

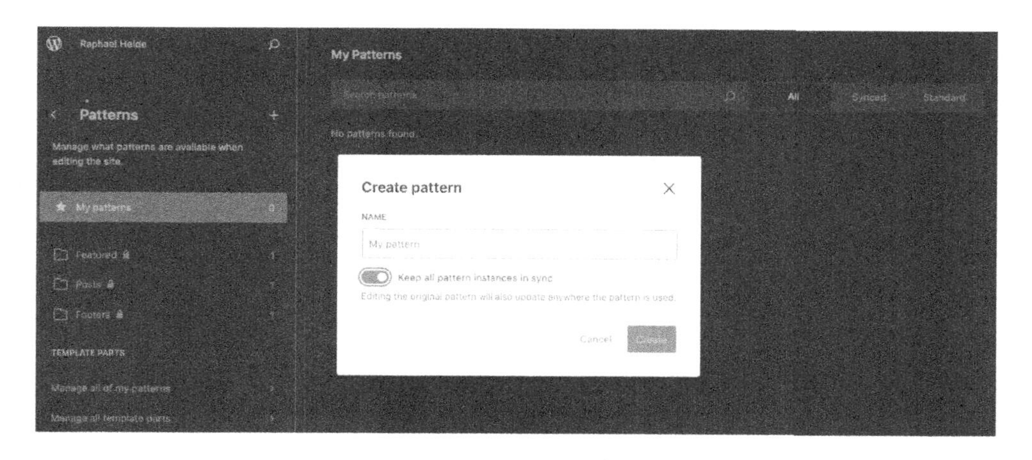

With these user-friendly features at your fingertips, you're poised to unlock the full potential of the Site Editor and design a website that reflects your unique vision and goals. The Patterns menu is your canvas, and it's time to let your creativity flow.

Step-by-step:

1 - In the Patterns menu, select the "Create pattern" option. A popup window will appear, allowing you to give your new pattern a name. This step is essential for easy reference and organization.

2 - If you prefer to create an unsynced pattern, simply disable the toggle switch labeled "Keep all pattern instances in sync." This choice provides the flexibility to make changes to the pattern without affecting the original.

3 - But the beauty of pattern creation doesn't stop within the Site Editor. Even in the general post or page editor, you have the power to craft and save patterns. Open the post or page you wish to work on, design it according to your vision, and choose the desired layout and content.

4 - In the toolbar, click on "Options." From there, navigate to the "Create pattern/reusable block" option. This opens up a world of possibilities. You can name your pattern and decide whether it should be a synced or unsynced pattern. The choice is yours. Now you can use your Pattern on blocks inside your posts or pages (we can see more on Posts and Pages: More Options).

The New Call an Action Function

WordPress automatically stores multiple revisions of your content as you work on it. This feature enables you to effortlessly revert to previous versions of your posts and pages.

In the same vein, with the introduction of WordPress 6.3, you can now access and manage revisions for your styles, making it simple to backtrack on any style changes.

To do this, just choose a style or block you wish to modify within the Styles panel.

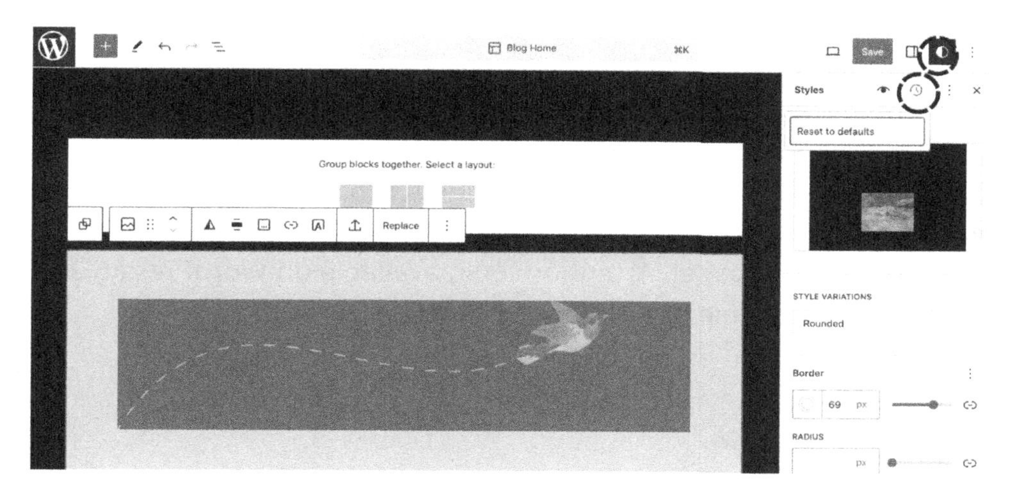

Click on the 'Revisions' button, and then opt for 'Revision history' to view and manage your style revisions.

Delete a Theme

If you no longer need a specific theme installed on your website, you can delete it from the "Themes" page. Locate the theme you want to remove, click on the "Theme Details" button, and then select the "Delete" link in the bottom-right corner of the window. Be cautious when deleting a theme, as it will remove all associated files and settings.

Widgets

Widgets in WordPress are small blocks of content or functionality that can be added to designated areas of a website, typically in the sidebar, footer, or other widget-ready areas. They provide an easy way to add various elements to your website without the need for coding or modifying theme files.

WordPress comes with a set of pre-built widgets that cover common functionalities, such as displaying recent posts, a search bar, a tag cloud, or a list of categories. These widgets can be accessed and managed through the "Appearance" > "Widgets" section in the WordPress admin panel. Attention: only available on WordPress 6.3 and 6.4 if your theme has a widget support.

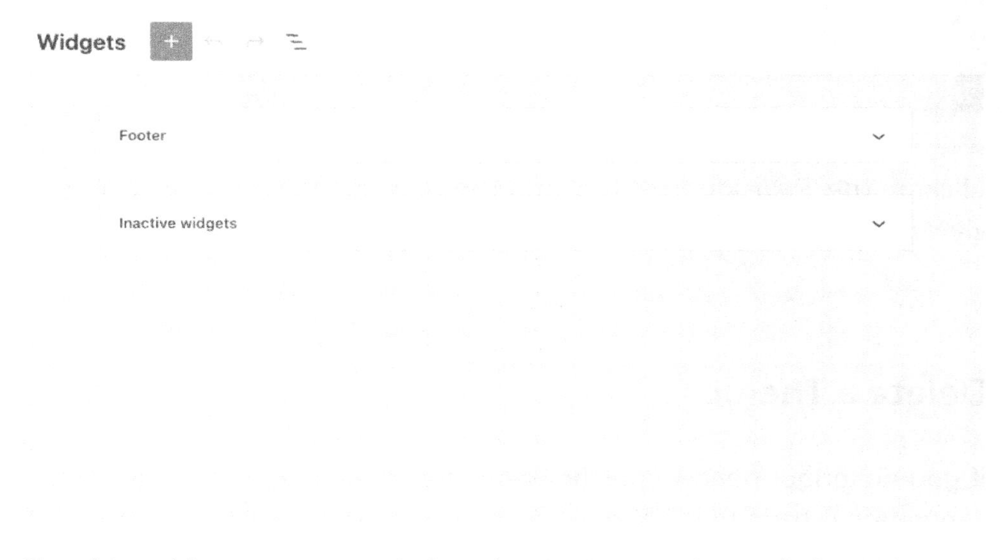

To add a widget to your website, simply drag and drop it from the available widgets area to the widget-ready area of your choice. Each widget has its own configuration options, allowing you to customize its settings. For example, you can specify the number of posts to display, the title of the widget, or select a category to show.

Some themes come with specific widgets, like Footer or Sidebar. You can add any information on widgets. Example: at Footer Widget you can add your site name and the year – MySite 2024. Or other information, like your address. Fell free to try what you want it.

In addition to the default widgets, many themes and plugins add their own custom widgets, extending the functionality and customization options. These widgets may provide features like social media integration, testimonials, contact forms, or custom content blocks.

Widget areas are theme-dependent, meaning that the available widget locations and their appearances can vary depending on the theme you're using. Some themes offer multiple widget areas, giving you flexibility in organizing and arranging the content on your website.

Widgets are highly customizable and can be rearranged or removed at any time. You can also control the visibility of widgets based on specific conditions, such as displaying a widget only on certain pages or for specific user roles.

Overall, widgets provide a user-friendly way to add functionality and content to your WordPress website. They allow you to enhance the appearance, organization, and usability of your site without the need for complex coding or development skills.

Menus

You just need to navigate in your page on Editor mode (Appearance -> Editor). Clique in your Menu (Top or Footer) and you can add or delete elements (links), logo, social links and more:

After you add or remove links and/or elements, you need to save.

For Your Information

It's important to navigate through the Editor and have a deep understanding of what it offers. It's worth noting that each theme contains an editor that may vary in its functionalities.

For the WordPress 6.3 editor to work correctly, it's necessary that a theme is updated for use in WordPress 6.3 or up. The vast majority of themes have been updated for compatibility with the latest WordPress update.

(Lesson 1)
First Website

Now it's time for Lesson 1. You can create your first website.

After you install your WordPress website, you need give a name and add basic information (check Settings Chapter).

Adding a New Theme

To add a new theme to your WordPress website, follow these steps:

a. Go to the "Appearance" section in your WordPress admin dashboard.

b. Click on "Themes" to access the themes page.

c. Click the "Add New" button.

d. Search for the Twenty Twenty-Tree theme or browse through the available themes.

e. Once you find the Twenty Twenty-Tree theme, click the "Install" button.

f. After the installation is complete, click the "Activate" button to make it the active theme for your website.

Activating the Theme

To activate the Twenty Twenty-Tree theme or any other theme, follow these steps:

a. Go to the "Appearance" section in your WordPress admin dashboard.

b. Click on "Themes" to access the themes page.

c. Find the Twenty Twenty -Tree theme in the list of installed themes.

d. Click the "Activate" button below the theme's details.

e. The Twenty Twenty-Tree theme is now active, and your website will reflect its design and layout.

Creating an "About Me" Page

To create an "About Me" page on your WordPress website, follow these steps:

a. Go to the "Pages" section in your WordPress admin dashboard.

b. Click on “Add New” to create a new page.

c. Give the page a title, such as “About Me”.

d. Write about yourself in the content area, sharing information and details you want to include.

e. Customize the page using the available formatting options.

f. Once you’re satisfied, click the “Publish” button to make the page live on your website.

Creating a “Blog” Page

To create a “Blog” page on your WordPress website, follow these steps:

a. Go to the “Pages” section in your WordPress admin dashboard.

b. Click on “Add New” to create a new page.

c. Give the page a title, such as “Blog“.

d. You don’t need to add any content to the page.

e. Once you’re done, click the “Publish” button to make the page live on your website.

Creating a Post

To create a post for your WordPress website, follow these steps:

a. Go to the "Posts" section in your WordPress admin dashboard.

b. Click on "Add New" to create a new post.

c. Give the post a title "My Lesson" and write about your lesson.

d. Once you're satisfied with your post, click the "Publish" button to make it live on your website.

Changing Home Page Display

To change the home page display settings on your WordPress website, follow these steps:

a. Go to the "Settings" section in your WordPress admin dashboard.

b. Click on "Reading" to access the reading settings.

c. Under the "Your homepage displays" section, select the "A static page" option.

d. Choose the "About Me" page from the dropdown menu for the "Homepage" option.

e. Choose the "Blog" page from the dropdown menu for the "Posts page" option.

f. Save your changes.

g. Now, your website's home page will display the content from the "About Me" page, and the blog posts will appear on the designated "Blog" page.

(15)
Posts and Pages: More Functions

In this chapter, we will explore additional functions and features you can use when creating posts and pages in WordPress. These functionalities will help you enhance the formatting, appearance, and interactivity of your content.

Adding a New Text with Gutenberg

To add a new text block using the Gutenberg editor, follow these steps:

a. Open the Gutenberg editor for a post or page.

b. Click on the "+" icon to add a new block.

c. Search for the "Text" block or find it in the "Common Blocks" section.

d. Click on the "Text" block to add it to your content.

e. Start typing or paste your desired text into the block.

Transforming Text into Heading, List, or Quote

With Gutenberg, you can easily transform your text into different formats. Here's how:

a. Select the text you want to transform.

b. In the block's toolbar, you will find options to change the text format.

c. Click on the appropriate button to transform the text into a heading, list, or quote.

Adding a Button

A button in a website is a graphical element that is designed to be clicked or tapped by users, triggering a specific action or navigation. It is a visual representation of an interactive element that encourages users to take a specific action, such as submitting a form, making a purchase, navigating to another page, or initiating a download.

Buttons typically have a distinct appearance that differentiates them from other elements on the page. They are often rectangular or rounded in shape and contain text or icons that convey the intended action. Buttons can be styled with various colors, sizes, and effects to attract attention and make them visually appealing.

Buttons serve as calls-to-action, guiding users to perform desired actions and interact with the website. They are essential for user engagement, conversion rates, and overall usability. Well-designed buttons with clear labels and intuitive placement can improve the user experience and encourage users to take specific actions that align with the website's goals.

To add a button to your content using Gutenberg, follow these steps:

a. Add a new block and search for the "Button" block.

b. Click on the "Button" block to insert it into your content.

c. Customize the button's text, link, and appearance using the block settings in the sidebar.

Adding a Code

In the context of website development, a code refers to the programming instructions written in a specific programming language that defines the structure, behavior, and appearance of a website. It is a set of instructions that tells the web browser how to render and display the web pages to the users.

You can use a code structure. But remember: WordPress is a CMS that makes your life easier and you don't need to know so much about code.

Code structure looks like:

```
<h1> My First Heading </h1>
<p> My first paragraph. </p>
```

The HTML element is everything from the start tag to the end tag. Some tags:

<h1> ... </h1>

Heading 1

<h2> ... </h2>

Heading 2

<h3> ... </h3>

Heading 3

<h4> ... </h4>

Heading 4

<h5> ... </h5>

Heading 5

<h6> ... </h6>

Heading 6

<p> ... </p>

Paragraph

<p style="color:blue;"> ... </p>

Text color blue

<a href=”your-link”> ... </a>

Link

<img src=”your-image.jpg”>

Image

<img src=” your-image.jpg “ width=”500” height=”600”>

Image with size in pixel

To add a code block to your content, follow these steps:

a. Add a new block and search for the “Code” block.

b. Click on the “Code” block to insert it into your content.

c. Enter or paste your code into the block.

d. Optionally, select the programming language for syntax highlighting.

Changing Columns and Stacking in Mobile

With Gutenberg’s column block, you can create multi-column layouts. Here’s how to adjust columns for mobile:

a. Add a column block to your content.

b. Select the block and navigate to the block settings in the sidebar.

c. Adjust the column layout by adding or removing columns.

d. In the block settings, enable the "Stack on Mobile" option to change the column layout for mobile devices.

Column Settings

When working with columns, you have additional settings to customize their appearance:

a. Select the column block and navigate to the block settings.

b. Adjust the column width by dragging the column handle.

c. Customize the column background, padding, and other styling options.

Aligning Text

To align text within a block, follow these steps:

a. Select the block containing the text.

b. In the block's toolbar, click on the alignment options to align the text left, center, right, or justify.

Formatting Text

Gutenberg provides various text formatting options in its toolbar:

a. To make text bold, select the text and click on the "B" button.

b. To italicize text, select the text and click on the "I" button.

c. To add a link to text, select the text and click on the chain icon and enter the URL.

d. To insert an inline image, click on the image icon and select an image from your media library.

e. To add keyboard input styling, click on the "Keyboard Input" icon.

Additional Formatting Options

Gutenberg offers several more formatting options:

a. To strikethrough text, select the text and click on the "Strikethrough" icon.

b. To subscript text, select the text and click on the "Subscript" icon.

c. To superscript text, select the text and click on the "Superscript" icon.

Typography (Size in Pixels)

In Gutenberg, you have the ability to adjust the font size of your text using pixel values. Here's how:

a. Select the text block or paragraph you want to modify.

b. In the block's toolbar, locate the font size options.

c. Click on the font size dropdown and select the desired pixel value.

Adding an Image Block

To insert an image into your content using Gutenberg, follow these steps:

a. Add a new block and search for the "Image" block.

b. Click on the "Image" block to add it to your content.

c. Choose an image from your media library or upload a new one.

d. Customize the image settings, such as alignment, size, and caption, using the block options.

Adding a Column Block

Gutenberg allows you to create multi-column layouts. Here's how to add a column block:

a. Add a new block and search for the "Columns" block.

b. Click on the "Columns" block to insert it into your content.

c. Customize the column layout by adding or removing column blocks.

d. Each column block can contain different content elements.

Adjusting Column Settings

To customize the appearance and behavior of the column block, follow these steps:

a. Select the column block you want to modify.

b. In the block's settings panel, adjust the column width, gap, and alignment.

c. Experiment with different settings to achieve your desired layout.

Adding a New Block Group

Gutenberg allows you to group blocks together for easier management. Here's how to create a block group:

a. Select the blocks you want to group by clicking and dragging over them.

b. In the block's toolbar, click on the "Group" button.

c. The selected blocks will now be grouped together, and you can move or modify them as a single unit.

Adding a New Heading Block

To create a heading using Gutenberg, follow these steps:

a. Add a new block and search for the "Heading" block.

b. Click on the "Heading" block to insert it into your content.

c. Choose the desired heading level (e.g., H1, H2, etc.) and enter your heading text.

Adding a List Block

To create a list using Gutenberg, follow these steps:

a. Add a new block and search for the "List" block.

b. Click on the "List" block to add it to your content.

c. Choose the list type (bulleted or numbered) and enter your list items.

Adding a Preformatted Block

If you want to display preformatted text or code snippets, use the preformatted block:

a. Add a new block and search for the "Preformatted" block.

b. Click on the "Preformatted" block to insert it into your content.

c. Enter your preformatted text or code within the block.

Adding a Pullquote Block

To highlight a quote or excerpt, use the pullquote block:

a. Add a new block and search for the "Pullquote" block.

b. Click on the "Pullquote" block to add it to your content.

c. Enter the quote or excerpt within the block.

Adding a Table Block

To create a table within your content, follow these steps:

a. Add a new block and search for the “Table” block.

b. Click on the “Table” block to insert it into your content.

c. Customize the table by adding or removing rows and columns.

d. Enter your content into the table cells.

Adding a Verse Block

If you want to display poetry or verse, use the verse block:

a. Add a new block and search for the “Verse” block.

b. Click on the “Verse” block to insert it into your content.

c. Enter your poetry or verse within the block.

The New 6.3 and 6.4 Blocks

The block editor in WordPress 6.3 introduces two new blocks for your convenience.

Footnotes Block

Footnotes serve as a convenient method for referencing resources at the bottom of your articles. Previously, WordPress users had to create footnotes manually or rely on external plugins to incorporate them.

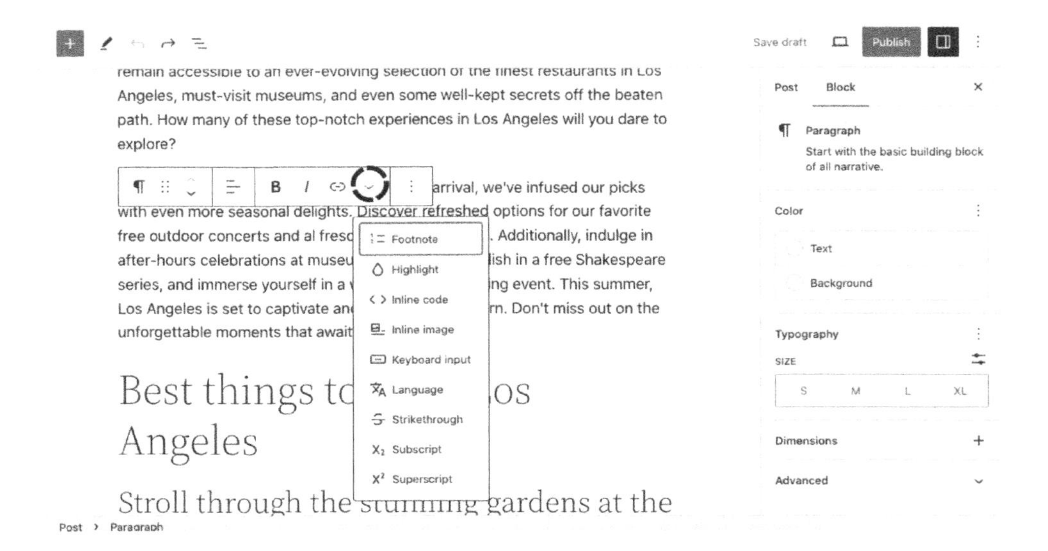

With the release of WordPress 6.3, adding footnotes is easier than ever. You can now seamlessly integrate footnotes into your content by selecting the 'Footnote' option from the three-dot menu in the toolbar. This new Footnotes block streamlines the process, making your content creation more efficient and user-friendly.

Details Block

The Details block is a versatile tool that allows you to hide content, requiring users to click on an item to reveal the hidden information.

Adding a Details block is straightforward. Begin by inserting the Details block and inputting the content you wish to display initially. Beneath that, you can provide the content that will be unveiled when users click on the visible portion.

Using the Details block, you have the flexibility to hide various types of content, such as paragraphs, images, media, or blocks added by plugins, and more. Additionally, you can combine multiple Details blocks to craft engaging features like FAQ sections, trivia questions, informative panels, and much more.

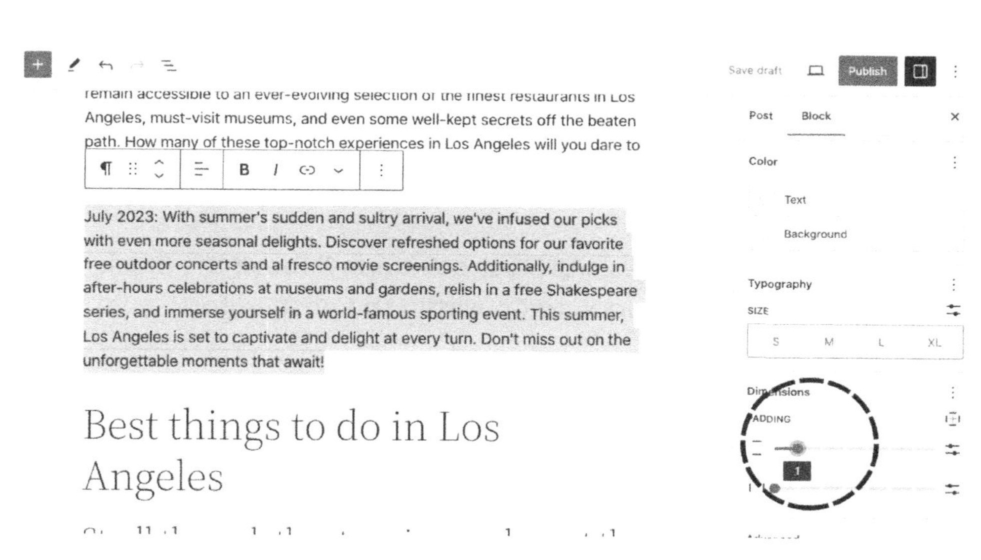

Enhanced Padding and Margin Tools

Previously, when users unlinked padding and margin settings, these tools occupied a substantial amount of space on the screen.

In WordPress 6.3, the new padding and margin tools have been redesigned to occupy significantly less screen space, providing a more user-friendly and efficient editing experience.

Select Aspect Ratio for Your Images

In WordPress 6.3, users can now choose the aspect ratio in which an image is displayed. This feature eliminates the need to manually resize and crop images, allowing users to pick an aspect ratio that ensures a consistent and appealing appearance across various devices.

Improved Top Toolbar

WordPress includes a toolbar positioned above the block you're currently working on within the post editor.

Furthermore, you now have the option to relocate the toolbar to the top of the screen, offering a cleaner and more streamlined editing environment.

Enable the top toolbar for a more efficient editing experience. Previously, the top toolbar appeared just below the main toolbar, consuming extra screen space and affecting the overall aesthetics.

With WordPress 6.3, the top toolbar has been revamped for improved accessibility and ease of use, making your editing tasks more convenient and visually pleasing.

By exploring and utilizing these various blocks and functions in Gutenberg, you can create dynamic and visually appealing posts and pages that engage your audience. Experiment with different options to discover the possibilities and make your content stand out.

(16)
Image Settings in a Page or Post

Images play a crucial role in enhancing the visual appeal of your WordPress pages or posts. Understanding the various image settings available can help you customize and optimize your images to create a compelling user experience. In this chapter, we'll explore the different image settings and their functionalities within WordPress.

Applying Styles

To add styles to your image, follow these steps:

a. Select the image block in the Gutenberg editor.

b. In the block settings panel, navigate to the "Styles" tab.

c. Choose from the available predefined styles or create custom styles using CSS.

Adding Alternative Text

Alternative text (alt text) provides a textual description of the image for accessibility purposes. To add alt text to an image, follow these steps:

a. Select the image block in the editor.

b. In the block settings panel, locate the “Alternative Text” field.

c. Enter a concise and descriptive text that represents the image content.

Changing Image Size

To adjust the display size of an image, follow these steps:

a. Select the image block in the editor.

b. In the block settings panel, navigate to the “Image Size” options.

c. Choose from the available size options to resize the image.

Changing Image Dimensions

To modify the dimensions (width and height) of an image, follow these steps:

a. Select the image block in the editor.

b. In the block settings panel, go to the “Image Dimensions” section.

c. Adjust the width and height values to resize the image accordingly.

Title Attribute

The “title” attribute in an image is important because it provides additional information about the image. When a user hovers their mouse over an image, the “title” attribute text is typically displayed as a tooltip or a small pop-up box, depending on the web browser or platform.

To add a title attribute to an image, follow these steps:

a. Select the image block in the editor.

b. In the block settings panel, locate the "Title Attribute" field.

c. Enter the desired title text for the image.

HTML Anchor

An HTML anchor allows you to create a link that jumps to a specific section on the page. To add an HTML anchor to an image, follow these steps:

a. Select the image block in the editor.

b. In the block settings panel, find the "Advanced" tab.

c. Enter a unique ID in the "HTML Anchor" field to create the anchor.

Aligning the Image

To align the image within the content, follow these steps:

a. Select the image block in the editor.

b. In the block settings panel, navigate to the "Alignment" options.

c. Choose the desired alignment, such as left, center, or right.

Adding a Caption

To add a caption to an image, follow these steps

a. Select the image block in the editor.

b. In the block settings panel, locate the "Caption" field.

c. Enter the desired caption text for the image.

Inserting a Link

To add a hyperlink to an image, follow these steps:

a. Select the image block in the editor.

b. In the block settings panel, find the "Link Settings" section.

c. Enter the URL you want to link to in the "Link URL" field.

You can past your URL and in settings on right side after the URL, you can decide open the link when is clicked in a new tab.

Cropping an Image

WordPress allows you to crop images to specific dimensions. To crop an image, follow these steps:

a. Select the image block in the editor.

b. In the block settings panel, go to the "Crop Image" section.

c. Adjust the crop handles to select the desired portion of the image.

Adding Text Over an Image

To overlay text on an image, follow these steps:s

a. Select the image block in the editor.

b. In the block settings panel, navigate to the "Overlay" options.

c. Enable the "Text Overlay" feature and enter the desired text.

Applying Duotone Filter

The duotone filter applies a two-color overlay on an image, creating an artistic effect. To apply a duotone filter, follow these steps:

a. Select the image block in the editor.

b. In the block settings panel, locate the "Filters" tab.

c. Choose the desired colors for the duotone effect.

Replacing an Image

To replace an existing image with a new one, follow these steps:

a. Select the image block in the editor.

b. In the block settings panel, find the "Replace" button.

c. Upload or select the new image from the media library.

Duplicating an Image

To make a copy of an image block, follow these steps:

a. Select the image block in the editor.

b. In the block settings panel, locate the "Duplicate" option.

c. Click on the option to create a duplicate image block.

Inserting Before or After an Image

To insert a new block before or after an existing image, follow these steps:

a. Select the image block in the editor.

b. In the block settings panel, find the "Insert Before" or "Insert After" options.

c. Choose the block type you want to insert.

Locking an Image

Locking an image prevents accidental modifications. To lock an image block, follow these steps:

a. Select the image block in the editor.

b. In the block settings panel, locate the "Lock" option.

c. Enable the lock feature to prevent edits.

Removing an Image

To remove an image from your content, follow these steps:

a. Select the image block in the editor.

b. In the block settings panel, find the "Remove" button.

c. Click on the button to remove the image block.

Editing as HTML

Editing as HTML allows you to modify the image code directly:

a. Select the image block in the editor.

b. In the block settings panel, locate the "More Options" section.

c. Click on the "Edit as HTML" option to access the HTML code.

Creating a Reusable Block

To create a reusable block from an image, follow these steps:

a. Select the image block in the editor.

b. In the block settings panel, locate the "More Options" section.

c. Click on the "Add to Reusable Blocks" option to create a reusable block.

By understanding and utilizing these image settings in WordPress, you can effectively manage and enhance the visual elements of your pages and posts, creating engaging and visually appealing content for your audience. Experiment with different settings and features to find the perfect balance for your website's design.

(17) Comments

Comments play a significant role in engaging with your audience and fostering discussions on your WordPress website. In this chapter, we will explore the importance of comments, how to manage them effectively, and ways to prevent spam comments. Comments link is located on the left-hand side.

What are WordPress Comments?

Comments are user-generated responses to your posts or pages. They allow visitors to share their thoughts, ask questions, and interact with you and other readers. Each comment typically includes the commenter's name, email address, website (optional), and their message.

Why are Comments Important?

Comments provide valuable feedback, insights, and discussions. They allow readers to express their opinions, offer suggestions, and engage in meaningful conversations. Comments can help build a sense of community on your website and enhance the overall user experience.

Managing Comments

Edit Comments: You can edit comments to correct typos or remove sensitive information. Locate the comment in the WordPress admin area, click on the "Edit" link, make the necessary changes, and save the edited comment.

Approve Comments: When a new comment is submitted, it goes into the moderation queue for your review. You can approve comments that meet your guidelines and are relevant to the discussion.

Unapproved Comments: If you find a comment inappropriate or spammy, you can unapprove it to hide it from your website until further action is taken.

Reply to Comments: Engage with your audience by replying to comments. Click on the "Reply" button below a comment, enter your response, and save it. This encourages further conversation and shows that you value reader input.

Quick Edit Comments

Quick Edit allows you to make simple modifications to a comment without accessing the full edit screen. To use Quick Edit:

Locate the comment in the WordPress admin area.

Hover over the comment and click on the "Quick Edit" link.

Make the desired changes, such as editing the author's name or comment text.

Save the changes.

Spam Comments

Spam comments are unsolicited or irrelevant comments usually intended for promotional purposes. They can be detrimental to the user experience and your website's reputation. To prevent spam comments:

Use Anti-Spam Plugins: Install and activate anti-spam plugins like Akismet or Jetpack to automatically filter and block spam comments.

Enable Comment Moderation: Set up comment moderation to manually approve comments before they appear on your website.

Use CAPTCHA or reCAPTCHA: Integrate CAPTCHA or reCAPTCHA services to add an extra layer of protection against automated spam bots.

Configure Comment Settings: Adjust the comment settings in your WordPress dashboard to require user registration or enable comment moderation for specific scenarios.

By effectively managing comments, engaging with your audience, and implementing spam prevention measures, you can create an interactive and spam-free commenting environment on your WordPress website.

The reCAPTCHA is a widely used security measure on the internet designed to distinguish between human users and automated bots. It was initially developed by Google and has become a standard method for preventing spam, abuse, and unauthorized access on websites.

The primary purpose of reCAPTCHA is to protect websites from automated attacks, such as spam form submissions, brute force login attempts, and malicious activities. It accomplishes this by presenting users with tests or challenges that are easy for humans to solve but difficult for bots.

There are different versions of reCAPTCHA available:

> **reCAPTCHA v2 (checkbox):** This version presents users with a checkbox that they need to click to confirm they are not a robot. In some cases, users may also be prompted to solve a simple image-based puzzle.
>
> **reCAPTCHA v3 (invisible):** Unlike the checkbox version, reCAPTCHA v3 works behind the scenes without requiring any user interaction. It assigns a score to user behavior on a website, helping website owners identify and take action against suspicious or malicious activities.

Integrating reCAPTCHA into a WordPress website involves a few steps. Here's a general guide to help you get started:

> **Sign up for reCAPTCHA:** Visit the reCAPTCHA website (https://www.google.com/recaptcha) and sign up for an API key. You'll need a Google account to access the reCAPTCHA API.
>
> **Choose reCAPTCHA type:** reCAPTCHA offers two types: reCAPTCHA v2 (checkbox) and reCAPTCHA v3 (invisible). For most websites, reCAPTCHA v2 is recommended. It presents users with a checkbox to confirm they are not a robot.

reCAPTCHA v3 works in the background and assigns a score based on the user's behavior on the website.

Install a reCAPTCHA plugin: In your WordPress admin dashboard, go to "Plugins" and click on "Add New." Search for a reCAPTCHA plugin like "reCAPTCHA by Google" or "Contact Form 7 reCAPTCHA." Install and activate the plugin of your choice.

Configure the plugin: Once the plugin is activated, go to its settings page. Enter your reCAPTCHA API key (Site key and Secret key) that you obtained in step 1. Save the settings.

Enable reCAPTCHA on forms: Depending on the plugin you chose, you can enable reCAPTCHA for specific forms or globally on all forms. For example, if you're using Contact Form 7, go to its settings and look for the reCAPTCHA section. Enable reCAPTCHA and select the version (v2 or v3). Save the form settings.

Test reCAPTCHA: Visit your website and test the forms where you've enabled reCAPTCHA. You should see the reCAPTCHA widget (checkbox) or invisible integration in action. Complete the form and verify that the reCAPTCHA validation is working as expected.

Remember to test the user experience after integrating reCAPTCHA to ensure it doesn't hinder legitimate users from submitting forms. Adjust the reCAPTCHA settings if needed to find the right balance between security and user convenience.

(18)
Media

WordPress provides a dedicated Media section that allows you to manage and organize your website's media files, such as images, videos, and audio. In this chapter, we will explore how to access the Media section, add new media files, and understand the Media Library.

Locating the Media Link

The Media link is typically located in the WordPress admin panel's sidebar or top navigation menu, depending on the version and theme you are using. It is often represented by an icon resembling an image or camera. Clicking on this link will take you to the Media section.

Adding a New Media File

To add a new media file to your WordPress website, follow these steps:

a. Access the Media section by clicking on the appropriate link in the admin panel.

b. Look for the "Add New" button, usually located at the top of the page. Click on it.

c. You will be prompted to either upload files from your computer or select existing files from your media library.

d. If you choose to upload files, click on the "Select Files" button and browse your computer to locate the desired media file(s). Alternatively, you can drag and drop the files into the upload area.

e. WordPress will begin uploading the files, and you will see a progress indicator.

f. Once the upload is complete, you can add additional information to the media files, such as title, alt text, captions, and descriptions.

g. Click on the "Save" or "Insert into Post" button to finalize the upload and add the media file to your Media Library.

Media Librarys

The Media Library is where all your uploaded media files are stored. It provides a comprehensive overview and management interface for your media assets. In the Media Library, you can perform various actions, including:

- View thumbnails or details of media files.

- Search for specific files using keywords.

- Filter media files by date, type, or category.

- Edit media details, such as titles, alt text, and captions.

- Delete or permanently remove media files from your library.

- Bulk select and perform actions on multiple files simultaneously.

Locating Media Files on the Web Host

When you upload media files to your WordPress website, they are stored in a designated folder on your web host. The exact location of this folder may vary depending on your hosting provider and configuration. By default, media files are typically stored in the "wp-content/uploads" directory within your WordPress installation. However, it's worth noting that accessing and modifying these files directly through your web host is not recommended, as it may lead to complications or errors in your WordPress site.

To access the wp-content/uploads directory in WordPress, you have a few different options depending on your needs and technical expertise. Here are three common methods:

Using a File Transfer Protocol (FTP) Client:

Download and install an FTP client software like FileZilla or Cyberduck.

Connect to your web server using the FTP client by entering your FTP credentials (host, username, password, and port).

Once connected, navigate to the root directory of your WordPress installation.

Locate the wp-content folder and open it.

Inside the wp-content folder, you will find the uploads directory.

Double-click on the uploads directory to access it and view its contents.

Using cPanel or Similar Hosting Control Panels:

Log in to your web hosting control panel (cPanel, Plesk, or similar).

Look for the "File Manager" or "File Explorer" icon and click on it.

Navigate to the directory where your WordPress installation is located.

Open the wp-content folder.

Inside the wp-content folder, you will find the uploads directory. Click on it to access its contents.

Using a WordPress File Manager Plugin:

Install and activate a WordPress file manager plugin like "File Manager" or "WP File Manager".s

Once activated, the plugin will typically add a new menu item or section in your WordPress admin panel.

Locate the file manager section and navigate to the root directory of your WordPress installation.

Open the wp-content folder.

Inside the wp-content folder, you will find the uploads directory. Click on it to access its contents.

Please note that accessing the wp-content/uploads directory should be done with caution, as modifying or deleting files without proper knowledge can potentially break your website. It is recommended to create backups and consult with a developer if you are unsure about making changes in this directory.

You can access the wp-content/uploads directory using softwares for Windows, Mac or Linux, like, Nova, Coda Kit, Visual Studio, and more.

(Lesson 2) Creating a New Post and Adding Content

Create a New Post

a. Go to your WordPress admin dashboard.

b. Click on "Posts" in the left-hand menu.

c. Click on "Add New" to create a new post.

Title and Content

a. In the post editor, enter the title as "What is new?"

b. Add a text block in the editor.

c. Write about your day today, sharing your experiences or any interesting events.

Adding an Image

a. Click on the (+) button to add a new block.

b. Search for the "Image" block and select it.

c. Upload an image or choose one from the media library.

d. In the block settings panel, provide the alternative text for the image as "What is new".

Adding Text and Creating a Link

a. Add another text block below the image.

b. Write "More about me" or any other text you want.

c. Select the text you want to turn into a link.

d. Click on the link icon in the block toolbar.

e. In the link settings, choose "Page" and select your "About Me" page from the dropdown.

f. Save the changes.

Save and Publishs

a. Once you have finished adding content, click on the "Save Draft" button to save your progress.

b. Preview the post to ensure everything looks as intended.

c. If you are satisfied, click on the "Publish" button to make the post live on your website.s

By following these steps, you can create a new post titled "What is new?", add text about your day, insert an image with an alternative text, and include a text block with a link to your "About Me" page.

Now you can check online all modifications in your website.

(19)
SSL - Secure Sockets Layer

No we are starting go deeper on WordPress. In this chapter, we will explore SSL (Secure Sockets Layer) and its importance for WordPress websites. We will also discuss how to install an SSL certificate on a WordPress site and explore some free SSL options available.

What is SSL?

SSL stands for Secure Sockets Layer. It is a cryptographic protocol that provides secure communication over the internet. SSL ensures that data transmitted between a user's browser and a website's server remains encrypted and secure, protecting sensitive information such as login credentials, personal details, and payment information.

Importance of SSL for WordPress Websites

Having an SSL certificate is crucial for several reasons:

Security: SSL encrypts data, preventing unauthorized access

and interception of sensitive information.

Trust and Credibility: SSL certificates display trust indicators such as a padlock icon and HTTPS in the address bar, reassuring visitors that their connection is secure and the website can be trusted.

SEO Benefits: Search engines like Google prioritize websites with HTTPS in search rankings, giving SSL-enabled sites a competitive edge.

Compliance: SSL is necessary for compliance with data protection regulations, such as the General Data Protection Regulation (GDPR).

How to Install an SSL on WordPress

Remember, to install SSL, some server knowledge is required. However, the support service of your server provider can install SSL on your website.

To install an SSL certificate on your WordPress website, follow these general steps:

Choose an SSL Certificate: You can obtain an SSL certificate from a trusted certificate authority (CA) or through your web hosting provider. There are different types of SSL certificates available, such as Domain Validated (DV), Organization Validated (OV), and Extended Validation (EV). Choose the one that suits your needs.

Purchase or Acquire an SSL Certificate: If you opt for a paid SSL certificate, follow the instructions provided by the certificate authority to purchase and obtain the certificate. If you prefer a free SSL certificate, you can explore the options mentioned in the next section.

Generate a Certificate Signing Request (CSR): Some SSL providers or hosting control panels require you to generate a CSR. Follow their instructions to generate the CSR, which includes providing details about your domain and organization.

Install the SSL Certificate: Depending on your hosting environment, the process of installing the SSL certificate may vary. Most hosting providers offer a simplified SSL installation process through their control panels or dashboard. Follow the specific instructions provided by your hosting provider or refer to their documentation.

Update Your Website Settings: After installing the SSL certificate, update your WordPress website settings to ensure all URLs use the HTTPS protocol. Go to the WordPress admin panel, navigate to Settings -> General, and update the WordPress Address (URL) and Site Address (URL) fields to start with "https://" instead of "http://".

Free SSL Options

If you are looking for free SSL options, here are some popular choices:

Let's Encrypt: Let's Encrypt is a widely recognized and trusted CA that provides free SSL certificates. Many hosting providers offer seamless integration with Let's Encrypt, making it easy to obtain and install SSL certificates.

Cloudflare: Cloudflare offers a free SSL option called "Flexible SSL" that encrypts the connection between the visitor and Cloudflare's servers. It is relatively easy to set up and provides a basic level of security.

SSL For Free: SSL For Free is a service that allows you to generate and install SSL certificates for free. It provides a simplified process for obtaining SSL certificates without the need for technical expertise.

Remember to research and choose a reputable SSL provider to ensure the security and reliability of your SSL certificate.

By implementing SSL on your WordPress website, you can enhance security, build trust with visitors, improve search engine rankings, and comply with data protection regulations.

For Your Information

The process of installing SSL certificates can vary depending on your hosting environment and specific circumstances. It is recommended to refer to the documentation or support resources provided by your hosting provider for detailed instructions tailored to your situation.

(20) What is .htaccess?

The .htaccess file is a configuration file used by the Apache web server to control and modify the behavior of your website. It is a powerful tool that allows you to make various adjustments to your site's functionality, security, and performance.

The importance of the .htaccess file cannot be overstated. It enables you to customize and fine-tune your website's settings without the need to directly modify the server's main configuration files. This flexibility makes it an essential component for managing your website effectively.

One reason why the .htaccess file is hidden is due to its sensitive nature. It contains directives and rules that govern how your website behaves, including security measures, URL redirections, caching instructions, and more. By keeping it hidden, it helps prevent accidental modifications or unauthorized access by users who may not have the necessary knowledge or permissions to make changes.

To access the .htaccess file, you need to connect to your website's server using FTP (File Transfer Protocol) or a file manager provided by your hosting provider. Once connected, navigate to the root directory of your website, where you'll typically find the .htaccess file. It's worth noting that the .htaccess file is often hidden by default, so you may need to configure your FTP client or file manager to show hidden files.

While manually editing the .htaccess file can be a technical task, there are WordPress plugins available that simplify the process. These plugins provide a user-friendly interface within the WordPress dashboard, allowing you to update and manage the .htaccess file without needing to access the server directly. Some popular WordPress plugins for managing the .htaccess file include "WP Htaccess Editor," "All In One WP Security & Firewall," and "iThemes Security."

Sometimes, when your WordPress website is experiencing issues, one way to troubleshoot is by checking the .htaccess file.

Your .htaccess file needs to look like:

```
# BEGIN WordPress

RewriteEngine On

RewriteRule .* - [E=HTTP_AUTHORIZATION:%{HTTP:Authorization}]

RewriteBase /

RewriteRule ^index\.php$ - [L]

RewriteCond %{REQUEST_FILENAME} !-f

RewriteCond %{REQUEST_FILENAME} !-d
```

RewriteRule . /index.php [L]

END WordPress

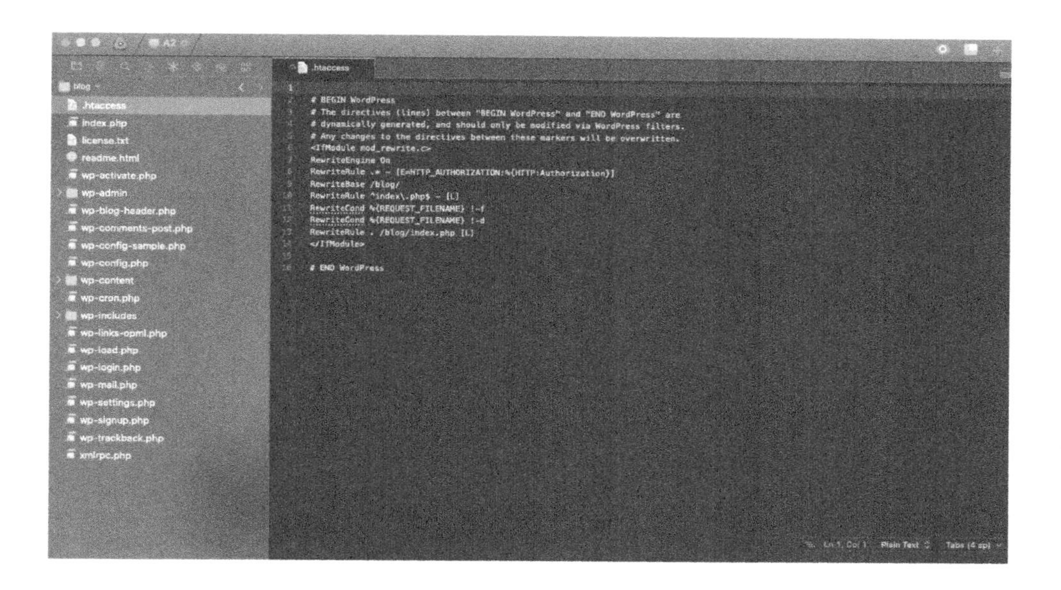

.htaccess file is on root of your WordPress. You can see in the image, my WordPress directory is raphaelheide.com/blog

(21)
Customizing a Theme

Customizing a theme allows you to personalize your WordPress website and make it unique to your brand or preferences. In this chapter, we will explore why customizing a theme is important, the level of difficulty involved, and how to perform specific customizations such as adding a logo and a footer. Additionally, we will discuss the differences between free and paid themes.

Importance of Customizing a Theme

Customizing a theme is crucial for establishing your website's identity and creating a cohesive branding experience. It allows you to align the design elements with your business goals, target audience, and overall aesthetics. By customizing a theme, you can make your website stand out from the crowd and create a memorable user experience.

Level of Difficulty

The complexity of customizing a theme can vary depending on your familiarity with web development and design concepts. Some themes come with built-in customization options that make the process simpler, while others may require more advanced coding knowledge. However, with the right resources and guidance, even beginners can learn to customize a theme effectively.

Adding Your Logo in a Theme

We talk before how to add your logo in the your website. Incorporating your logo into a theme helps in branding your website. Most WordPress themes provide options to upload and display your logo easily. We will guide you through the steps to add your logo, ensuring it appears prominently on your website's header or any other designated location.

Make sure you have a logo in good definition. To add a logo to your WordPress theme, follow these steps:

Prepare your logo: Make sure you have your logo image file ready in a suitable format, such as PNG or JPEG. Ideally, the logo should have a transparent background for seamless integration with the theme.

Log in to your WordPress admin panel: Enter your website's admin URL (e.g., www.yourwebsite.com/wp-admin/) and log in using your credentials.

Access the Theme Customizer: In the WordPress dashboard, go to "Appearance" and click on "Customize" (WordPress 5, 6.0, or 6.1) or ""Editor (WordPress 6.2, 6.3, or 6.4)" This will open the Theme Customizer, which allows you to make visual changes to your theme.

Locate the Logo settings: Depending on your theme, the location of the Logo settings may vary. Look for options like "Site Identity," "Header," or "Logo" within the Theme Customizer.

On Editor you need to click the logo place and add.

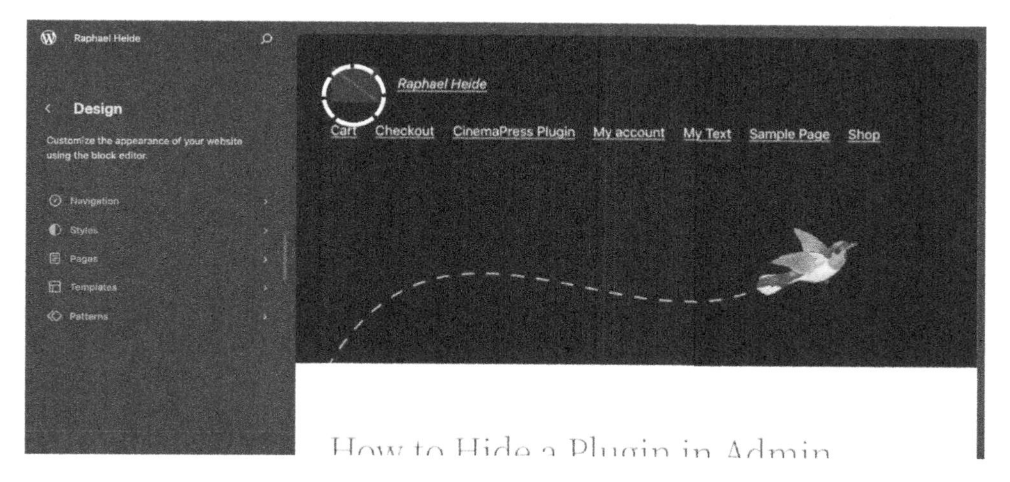

After you click:

Upload your logo: Within the Logo settings, you will typically find an option to upload your logo image. Click on the "Select Logo" or "Upload" button to choose your logo file from your computer and upload it to your website.

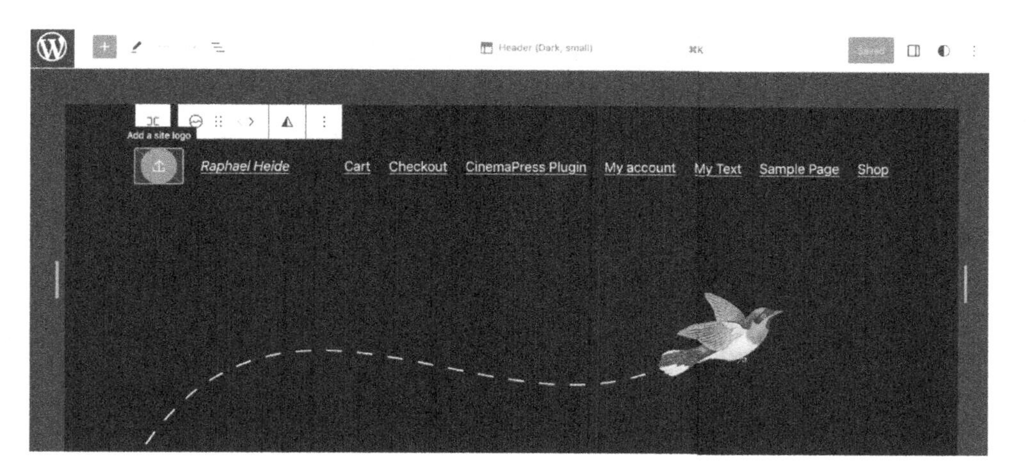

Adjust logo dimensions and position (if necessary): Some themes offer additional customization options for the logo, such as resizing or repositioning. If needed, use the provided settings to make any necessary adjustments to ensure your logo looks visually pleasing within the theme's header area.

Save and publish the changes: Once you are satisfied with the logo placement and settings, click on the "Save" or "Publish" button within the Theme Customizer to save your changes. The new logo will now appear on your website's front-end.

Note: If your theme does not have built-in logo settings or the option to upload a logo directly, you may need to customize the theme's header template files or consider using a plugin specifically designed for logo management.

A favicon, short for "favorite icon," is a small image or icon that represents a website or web page. It appears in the browser tab or window, next to the page title when a user visits the site. Favicon helps in branding and provides a visual identity for the website.

You can create a favicon using graphic design software like Adobe Photoshop, GIMP, or online favicon generators. Start with a square image and resize it to the appropriate favicon dimensions. Ensure that the design is clear and recognizable even at a small size.

Open the Site Editor by navigating to Appearance -> Editor in the WordPress dashboard. Hover your mouse over the area where you want to place the logo and click the insert block button (+).

Although you can add your favicon anywhere on the site, we recommend adding it to the header area.

Search for the Site Logo block in the search bar and select it to add it to your site.

Option to insert a favicon in the Gutenberg visual editor.

Click the Add a Site Logo button in the block to open the media library pop-up. Adding a site logo in WordPress.

Upload your image file or select it from the media library. Click Select.

WordPress media library pop-up, displaying a selected favicon file. You will see the favicon image in the site logo block. Click on the block and open its Settings in the top right corner of the editor.

Open the Settings section and activate the Use as site icon option. The settings section for the site logo block, with the option to use it as a site icon highlighted.

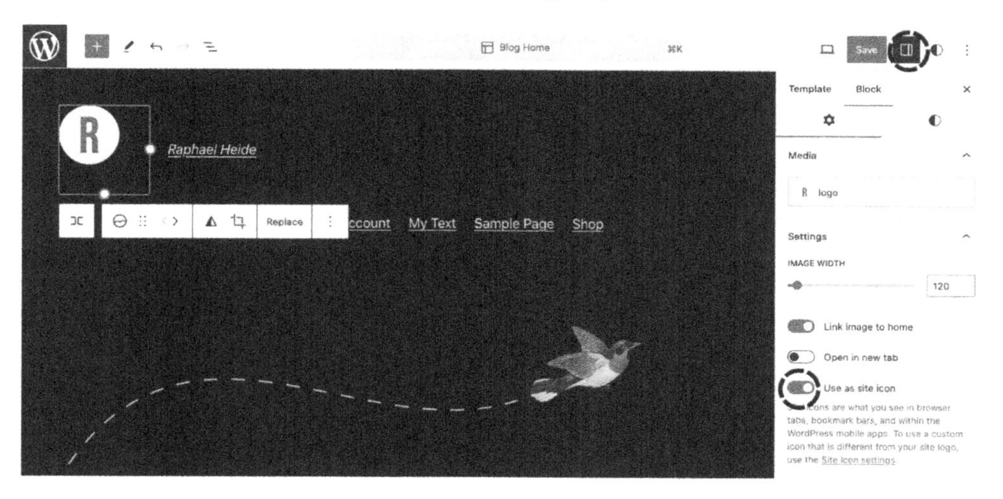

Click Save in the top right corner of the editor.

Your favicon will be displayed in your browser.

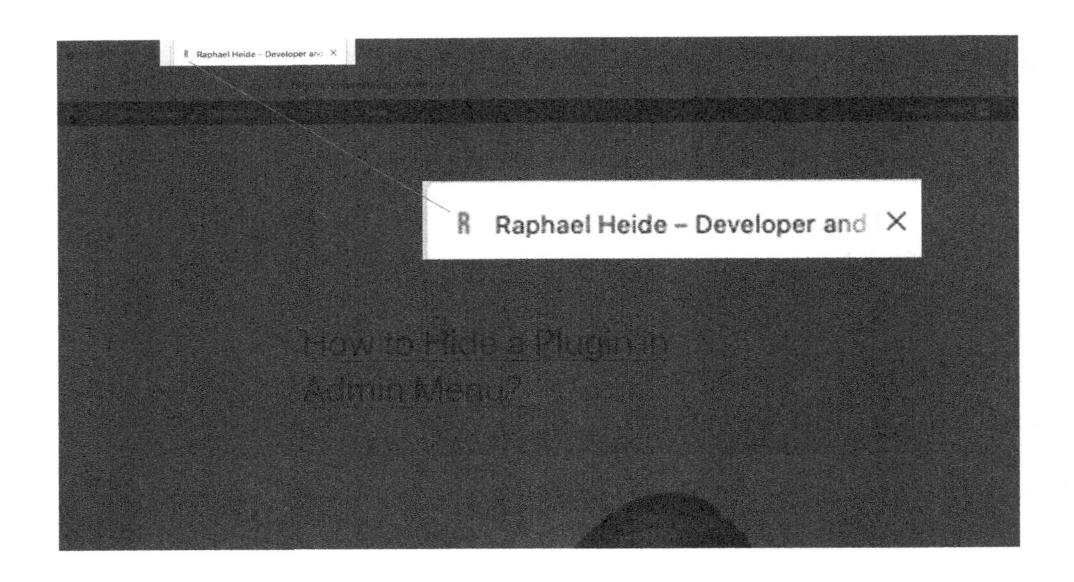

Adding a Footer in a Theme

The footer section of a website provides valuable information and additional navigation options. Customizing the footer allows you to include copyright notices, contact information, social media links, or other relevant content. We will explore how to modify the footer area to suit your requirements. In WordPress 6.2, 6.3, or 6.4, you will make the same steps of add a menu.

To add a footer to your WordPress theme in other versions:

Access the Theme Customizer: Log in to your WordPress admin panel and go to “Appearance” and click on “Eitor.” This will open the Theme Customizer, where you can make visual changes to your theme.

Locate the Footer settings: Depending on your theme, the location of the Footer settings may vary. Look for options like “Footer,” “Footer Widgets,” or “Bottom Bar” within the Theme Customizer.

Enable footer widgets: If your theme supports footer widgets, you may need to enable the footer widget area first. Look for a checkbox or toggle switch to enable the footer widgets.

Configure the footer widgets: Once the footer widgets are enabled, you can configure the number of widget areas or columns you want to display in the footer. Some themes offer multiple widget areas, allowing you to customize the layout of your footer.

Add widgets to the footer: After configuring the footer widget areas, go to "Appearance" and click on "Widgets" in the WordPress admin panel. You will see the available widget areas for your footer. Drag and drop the desired widgets from the left-hand side into the footer widget areas on the right-hand side.

Customize the footer text or copyright information: Some themes provide specific options to customize the footer text or copyright information. Look for settings related to the footer text within the Theme Customizer and update it with your desired content.

Save and publish the changes: Once you have added the widgets and customized the footer text, click on the "Save" or "Publish" button within the Theme Customizer to save your changes. The footer with the added widgets and text will now be visible on your website's front-end.

Free Themes vs. Paid Themes

WordPress offers a vast selection of both free and paid themes. Free themes provide a budget-friendly option to get started, but they may have limited customization options and may be used by many other websites. On the other hand, paid themes often offer more advanced features, extensive customization possibilities, and dedicated support. We will discuss the pros and cons of both options to help you make an informed decision.

Customizing a theme allows you to create a visually appealing and functional website tailored to your specific needs. Whether you choose to work with a free or paid theme, the ability to add your logo, modify the footer, and make other customizations will help your website stand out and leave a lasting impression on your visitors.

Child Theme

A child theme is a theme that inherits the functionality and styling of another theme, known as the parent theme. It allows you to make modifications to a theme without directly modifying the original theme's files. Instead, you create a separate folder containing only the files you want to customize, and WordPress will use those files in conjunction with the parent theme.

For Your Information

While child themes can be beneficial in certain situations, not all users necessarily need to use them. Here are a few reasons why many users may not require a child theme:

> **Using Pre-built Themes:** Many users opt for pre-built themes available in theme marketplaces or provided by theme developers. These themes are typically well-maintained and regularly updated by the developers. As a result, users can

safely update their themes without the need for a child theme. If customization is limited to the theme's built-in options or minor CSS changes, a child theme may not be necessary.

Minimal Customization: If the user's customization needs are minimal, such as changing colors, fonts, or simple CSS adjustments, these modifications can often be made using customizer options or using a custom CSS plugin. In such cases, a child theme may not be required as the changes can be applied directly to the main theme without the need for a separate child theme.

Temporary Modifications: In some cases, users may require temporary modifications to their theme for specific events or campaigns. In such situations, creating a child theme may not be necessary since the modifications will only be applied temporarily, and the main theme can be updated without affecting those changes.

Trust in Theme Updates: If users have confidence in the theme developer's ability to release regular updates that maintain compatibility with new WordPress versions and plugins, they may not feel the need for a child theme. Regular updates from theme developers ensure that bug fixes, security patches, and new features are implemented, allowing users to benefit from these updates without the need for a child theme.

Child themes are useful for several reasons:

Preserving customizations: If you make changes to a theme's files directly and then update the theme, your modifications may be lost. With a child theme, your customizations remain intact even when the parent theme is updated.

Modifying theme functionality: Child themes allow you to override specific functions or add new functions to extend the features of the parent theme. This can be done by creating a functions.php file in the child theme.

Customizing styling: You can modify the CSS styles of the parent theme by creating a style.css file in the child theme. Any changes you make will override the corresponding styles in the parent theme.

To create a child theme, you need to:

Create a new folder in the "wp-content/themes" directory of your WordPress installation. Give it a unique name, preferably related to the parent theme.

Inside the child theme folder, create a style.css file. In this file, you need to add a header comment that specifies the parent theme. The comment should look like this:

```
/*

Theme Name: My Child Theme

Template: parent-theme-folder-name

*/
```

Replace "My Child Theme" with the name of your child theme, and "parent-theme-folder-name" with the name of the parent theme's folder.

Optionally, you can create a functions.php file in the child theme folder to override or add new functions.

Activate the child theme in the WordPress admin panel under "Appearance" > "Themes." You should see your child theme listed, and you can activate it from there.

Once the child theme is activated, you can start customizing the theme by modifying the appropriate files within the child theme folder. Any changes you make will be reflected on your website while still maintaining the core functionality of the parent theme.

Using a child theme is a recommended approach for making customizations to a WordPress theme because it ensures your modifications are separate from the parent theme, making it easier to manage updates and maintain a clean codebase.

Remember

Creating a child theme in WordPress is not particularly difficult, especially if you have a basic understanding of HTML, CSS, and some familiarity with WordPress themes. The process involves following a few steps and requires editing some files, but it is a straightforward process. Here is an overview of the steps involved:

Create a new folder: You need to create a new folder in the "wp-content/themes" directory of your WordPress installation. Give it a unique name for your child theme.

Create a style.css file: Inside the child theme folder, create a style.css file. This file is where you will define the styles for your child theme. It should include a header comment that specifies the parent theme.

Specify the parent theme: In the style.css file, add a header comment that includes the Theme Name and Template fields. The Template field should contain the directory name of the parent theme.

Customize the child theme: You can now add your custom CSS styles and make modifications to the theme files in your child theme. Any changes you make to the files in the child theme will override the corresponding files in the parent theme.

Activate the child theme: Once your child theme is ready, you need to activate it in the WordPress admin panel under "Appearance" > "Themes." Your child theme should be listed there, and you can activate it.

While creating a basic child theme is relatively easy, the complexity can vary depending on the level of customization you want to achieve. If you have more advanced requirements, such as modifying template files or adding custom functionality, it may require a deeper understanding of PHP and WordPress theme development.

However, there are many resources available online, including tutorials, documentation, and forums, that can guide you through the process of creating a child theme. WordPress also has a developer-friendly community, so if you encounter any challenges, you can seek assistance from experienced developers.

Overall, creating a child theme is considered a best practice when customizing a WordPress theme, as it provides a safe and upgrade-friendly way to make modifications. With a little patience and willingness to learn, you can successfully create and customize your own child theme in WordPress.

(22) SEO - Boosting Your Website's Visibility

In the digital age, having a stunning WordPress website is not enough. You also need to ensure that your website can be easily found by search engines and potential visitors. That's where SEO (Search Engine Optimization) comes into play. In this chapter, we will explore the world of SEO and discover how you can optimize your WordPress website to improve its visibility and attract organic traffic.

Understanding SEO

Search Engine Optimization (SEO) is a multifaceted strategy that focuses on enhancing your website's content, structure, and technical elements to secure better rankings in search engine results pages (SERPs).

SEO plays a pivotal role in the digital landscape. It serves as the bedrock for attracting organic traffic to your website. By meticulously tailoring your online presence to match what search engines look for, you can significantly boost your visibility on the web. Moreover, SEO is instrumental in fortifying your website's credibility and authority in its niche.

In essence, SEO is not merely a technical endeavor; it's a dynamic and indispensable practice for businesses and individuals looking to thrive in the online sphere.

Making Your WordPress Website SEO Friendly

Keyword research: Identify relevant keywords related to your website's content and integrate them strategically throughout your posts and pages.

Optimizing title tags and meta descriptions: Craft compelling and keyword-rich title tags and meta descriptions to entice users to click on your website in search results.

Optimizing URL structure: Create SEO-friendly URLs that include relevant keywords and accurately describe the content of your pages.

A good page SEO-friendy:

If you want to have a page with a title "100 things to do in Las Vegas".

Your page URL structure would like "yourwebsite.com/100-things-to-do-in-las-vegas"

To change your permalink, check the Chapter Settings.

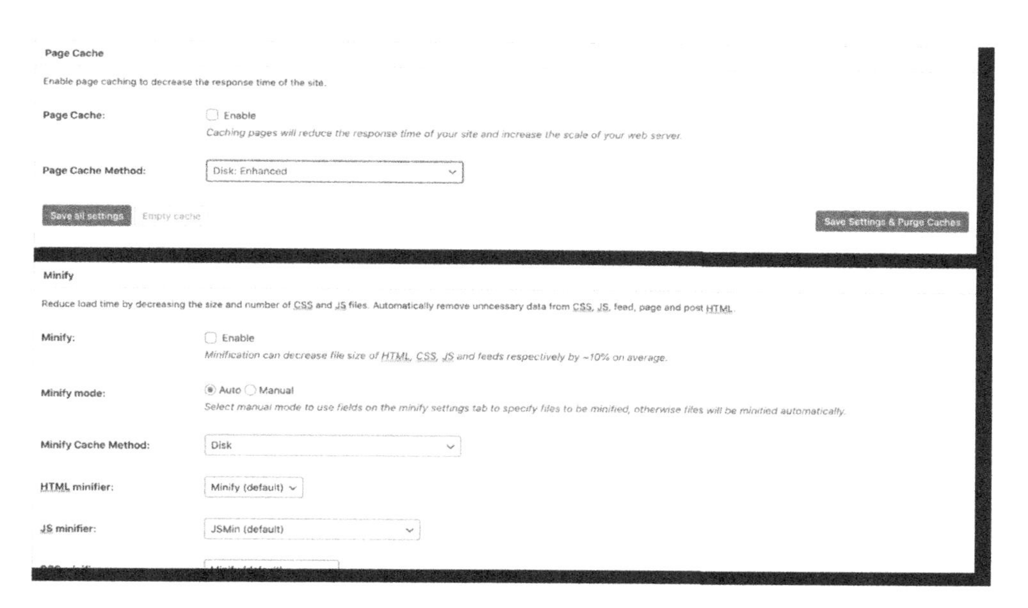

Improving website speed: Optimize your website's loading speed to provide a better user experience and improve search engine rankings. A cache plugin can significantly improve the performance and speed of your WordPress website by storing a temporary copy of your web pages, images, and other static content. When a user visits your site, the cache plugin serves the stored copy instead of generating the page from scratch, reducing the server load and improving the overall user experience.

Download a cache plugin. Here some cache plugins examples:

W3 Total Cache Plugin:

Improvements in search engine result page rankings, especially for mobile-friendly websites and sites that use SSL

At least 10x improvement in overall site performance (Grade A in WebPagetest or significant Google PageSpeed improvements) **when fully configured**

Improved conversion rates and "site performance" which affect your site's rank on google.com

"Instant" repeat page views: browser caching

Optimized progressive render: pages start rendering quickly and can be interacted with more quickly

Reduced page load time: increased visitor time on site; visitors view more pages

Improved web server performance; sustain high traffic periods

Up to 80% bandwidth savings when you minify HTML, minify CSS and minify JS files.

WP Fastest Cache Plugin:

Mod_Rewrite which is the fastest method is used in this plugin

All cache files are deleted when a post or page is published

Admin can delete all cached files from the options page

Admin can delete minified css and js files from the options page

Block cache for specific page or post with Short Code

Cache Timeout – All cached files are deleted at the determinated time

Cache Timeout for specific pages

Enable/Disable cache option for mobile devices

Enable/Disable cache option for logged-in users

SSL support

CDN support

Cloudflare support

Preload Cache – Create the cache of all the site automatically

Exclude pages and user-agents

WP-CLI cache clearing

Proxy Cache – Varnish Cache Integration to clear proxy cached content automatically when the cache created by WP Fastest Cache is cleared

Optimizing images: Compress and optimize images to reduce their file size without compromising quality, and add descriptive alt tags to improve SEO. Image optimizer helps optimize and compress the images on your website. It automatically reduces the file size of your images without sacrificing quality, resulting in faster page loading times and improved website performance.

You can download EWWW Image Optimizer Plugin. Sometimes you can reduce images in 80%, making your website faster.

Creating high-quality content: Craft informative, engaging, and well-structured content that provides value to your audience and aligns with their search intent.

Implementing internal linking: Include relevant internal links within your content to improve website navigation and enhance SEO.

SEO Plugins for WordPress

You can find free and paid SEO Plugins. For download SEO Plugins, check the chapter Plugins and search for SEO.

Free SEO plugins: Explore popular free SEO plugins like Yoast SEO, All in One SEO Pack, and Rank Math to optimize your website's SEO settings and analyze your content.

Paid SEO plugins: Consider premium SEO plugins like SEMrush, Ahrefs, and Moz Pro for advanced SEO features and comprehensive analytics.

Using SEO Plugins

Setting up SEO plugins: Install and activate your preferred SEO plugin, and configure its settings according to your website's requirements.

On-page SEO analysis: Use the SEO plugin to analyze your posts and pages for keyword optimization, readability, meta tags, and more.

XML sitemaps: Generate XML sitemaps using the SEO plugin to help search engines crawl and index your website effectively.

Social media integration: Some SEO plugins offer social media integration features, allowing you to optimize your website's visibility on social platforms.

Word Count and SEO

Word count guidelines: While there is no fixed rule, longer, comprehensive content tends to perform better in search results. Aim for at least 300-500 words for blog posts and 1,000+ words for in-depth articles.

Quality over quantity: Remember that content quality and relevance are equally important. Focus on providing valuable information to your audience rather than solely aiming for a specific word count.

Using Yoast SEO Plugin

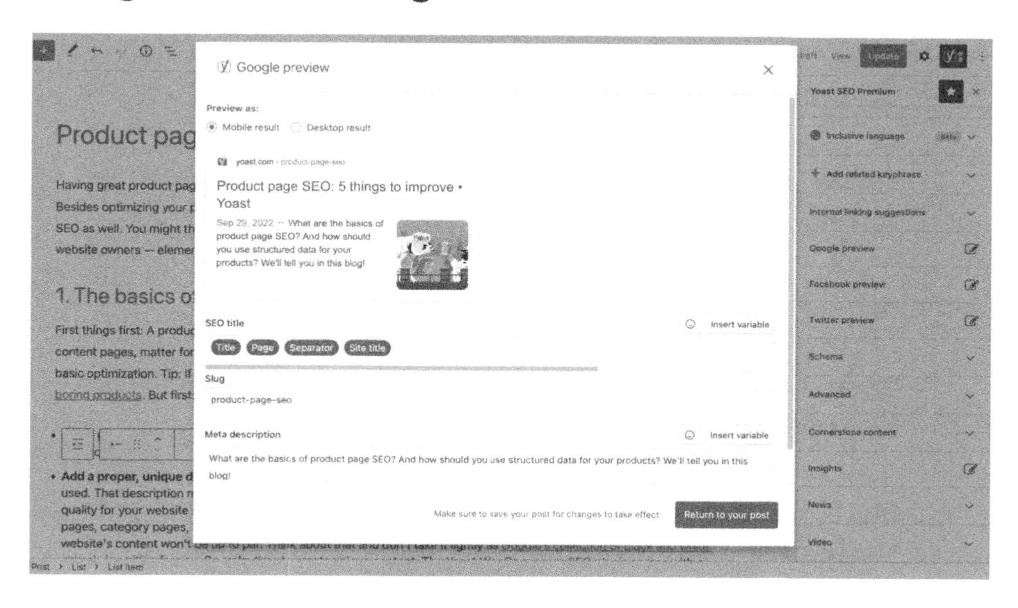

Yoast SEO is a popular WordPress plugin that helps you optimize your website for search engines. Here's a step-by-step guide on how to use Yoast SEO effectively.

Install and activate Yoast SEO:

Go to your WordPress dashboard.

Navigate to "Plugins" and click on "Add New."

Search for "Yoast SEO" in the search bar.

Click "Install Now" next to the Yoast SEO plugin.

After installation, click "Activate" to activate the plugin.

Configure Yoast SEO settings:

Upon activation, you'll see a new menu item called "SEO" in your WordPress dashboard.

Click on "SEO" and go to the "General" tab.

Follow the on-screen instructions to configure the basic settings for your website.

Optimize individual posts and pages:

When creating or editing a post or page, scroll down to the Yoast SEO box below the content editor.

Start by entering your focus keyword or keyphrase for that specific page or post.

Yoast SEO will provide an analysis and give you recommendations to improve your content's SEO.

Pay attention to the SEO analysis section, which provides suggestions for optimizing your content, including title tags, meta descriptions, headings, internal and external links, and keyword usage.

Use the content analysis feature to check if your content meets the recommended SEO guidelines.

Customize your SEO settings:

> Access the Yoast SEO settings by clicking on "SEO" in your WordPress dashboard and selecting "Search Appearance."
>
> In this section, you can customize how your website's titles, meta descriptions, and other elements appear in search engine results.
>
> You can also set up XML sitemaps, social media metadata, and other advanced settings based on your specific requirements.

Utilize additional features:

> Yoast SEO offers various advanced features, including breadcrumb navigation, schema markup, and bulk editing for SEO settings.
>
> Explore these features based on your website's needs and follow the plugin's documentation and guides for a more detailed understanding.

Stay updated with Yoast SEO:

> Yoast SEO regularly releases updates to improve functionality and address any security or compatibility issues.

Keep an eye on updates and ensure you are using the latest version of the plugin for optimal performance.

For Your Information

Remember, Yoast SEO is a powerful tool, but it's important to use it as a guide rather than solely relying on its recommendations. Combine its insights with your knowledge and understanding of your target audience to create valuable and optimized content that resonates with both search engines and users.

(23)
XML, Sitemap, Google Webmaster

XML, Sitemaps, and Google Webmaster are essential tools for optimizing your website's SEO. In this chapter, we'll explore their functions and how to utilize them effectively.

What is XML for SEO?

XML (Extensible Markup Language) is a format used to structure and organize data on the internet.

In the context of SEO, XML is used to create a sitemap, which helps search engines understand the structure and content of your website.

What is a Sitemap?

A sitemap is a file that lists all the pages, posts, and other content on your website, along with their hierarchical structure. It helps search engine crawlers navigate and index your site more efficiently.

How to Create an XML/Sitemap file for SEO?

There are various methods and plugins available to generate XML sitemaps for your WordPress website: Yoast SEO, All in One SEO Pack, and Google XML Sitemaps are popular plugins that simplify the process of creating a sitemap.

Install and activate one of these plugins, then follow the plugin's settings to generate your XML sitemap.

You can make your own Sitemap. Just search online for "Sitemap generator". On the website, type your Wordpress website and download the xml file. Upload for your web hosting (on root) - looking how to upload a file on Chapter 5.

What is Google Webmaster?

Google Webmaster, now known as Google Search Console, is a free tool provided by Google for website owners. It offers insights into your website's performance in search results and provides various SEO-related features.

Having a Google Webmaster Account allows you to monitor your website's indexing status, search visibility, and performance in Google search results.

It provides valuable data and reports that can help you improve your website's SEO.

How to set up a Google Webmaster Account

Visit the Google Search Console website and sign in using your Google account.

Follow the instructions to verify ownership of your website by adding a verification code or a DNS record.

For Your Information

To add the verification code, you need login in your web hosting. Check the "Chapter How to Setup a Web Server". You can ask your web hosting company to setup your DNS record.

After your update your DNS record, takes until 2 hours for information be online.

How to set up WordPress on Google Webmaster

After verifying ownership, you can add your website to Google Webmaster by clicking the "Add Property" button.

Enter your website's URL and follow the on-screen instructions to verify the ownership.

Functions of Google Webmaster

Google Webmaster offers various tools and features to help you monitor and improve your website's performance in search results.

It provides data on search queries, crawl errors, backlinks, mobile usability, and more.

How to Upload your Sitemap to your web hosting

Once you have generated your XML sitemap using a plugin, you can access the file from your web hosting account.

Connect to your web hosting via FTP or use the file manager provided by your hosting provider.

Upload the XML sitemap file to the root directory of your website.

How to submit your Sitemap to Google Webmaster

In Google Webmaster, select your website property and navigate to the "Sitemaps" section.

Click on "Add a new sitemap" and enter the URL of your XML sitemap. Exemple: mywebsite.com/sitemap.xml (sitemap.xml is the name of file your upload on server).

Submit the sitemap, and Google will start crawling and indexing the pages listed in your sitemap.

How to submit a page manually to Google Webmaster

In Google Webmaster, go to the "URL Inspection" tool.

Enter the URL of the specific page you want to submit and click "Enter."

Click on the "Request Indexing" button to request Google to crawl and index the page.

By utilizing XML, sitemaps, and Google Webmaster effectively, you can enhance your website's visibility in search results and improve its overall SEO performance. These tools provide valuable insights and control over how search engines interpret and index your content, ultimately driving more organic traffic to your website.

(24)
How to Use Social Networks in Your WordPress Website

Social networks have become an integral part of our online lives, allowing us to connect, share, and engage with others on a global scale. In this chapter, we will explore how to leverage social networks to enhance your WordPress website's reach and engagement.

What are Social Networks and Examples

Social networks are online platforms that enable users to connect, share content, and interact with others.

Examples of popular social networks include Facebook, Instagram, X (former-Twitter), LinkedIn, Pinterest, and YouTube.

Business Social Networks

Business-oriented social networks cater specifically to professionals and organizations.

LinkedIn is a prominent example of a business social network, offering networking opportunities, job postings, and industry insights.

How to Add a Social Network Plugin to Your WordPress Website

WordPress offers a wide range of plugins that allow you to integrate social network features into your website seamlessly.

Install a social media plugin such as "Social Icons," "AddToAny Share Buttons," or "Jetpack" to enable social sharing, like buttons, and follow icons on your website.

Configure the plugin settings to customize the appearance and behavior of the social network buttons.

Social Networks Examples

Facebook: The largest social network, ideal for connecting with a broad audience and sharing various types of content.

Instagram: A visually-oriented platform, perfect for sharing images and short videos to engage with your audience.

X (former-Twitter): A microblogging platform known forits concise updates, ideal for sharing news, updates, and engaging in real-time conversations.

LinkedIn: A business-focused network, great for networking, professional branding, and sharing industry-related content.

Pinterest: A platform centered around visual discovery, allowing users to share and discover ideas through "pins" and boards.

YouTube: The leading video-sharing platform, ideal for hosting and sharing video content, tutorials, and product demonstrations.

By integrating social networks into your WordPress website, you can expand your online presence, encourage social engagement, and drive more traffic to your site. Remember to choose social networks that align with your target audience and content strategy to maximize the benefits of these platforms.

To add social sharing buttons to your WordPress

Install a Social Sharing Plugin: In your WordPress admin dashboard, navigate to "Plugins" on the sidebar and click on "Add New." Search for a social sharing plugin like "Simple Share Buttons Adder," "Social Warfare," or "AddToAny." Choose a plugin that suits your needs and has good reviews. Click "Install" and then "Activate" to enable the plugin.

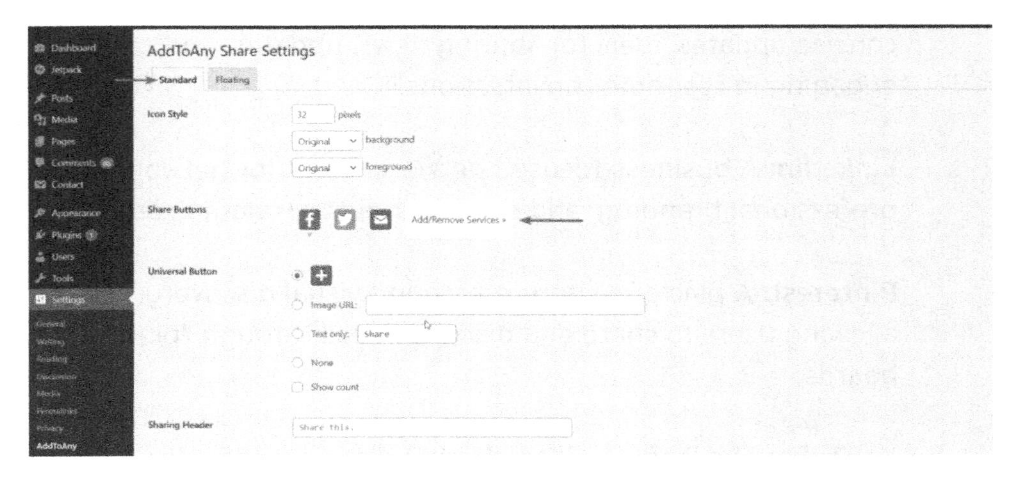

Configure the Social Sharing Plugin: Once the plugin is activated, you will usually find a new menu item in your WordPress dashboard called "Sharing" or something similar. Go to the plugin's settings page to configure the social sharing buttons.

Select the social media platforms you want to include in the sharing buttons.

Customize the appearance, placement, and style of the buttons.

Choose whether to display share counts or other additional features.

Configure the button labels, icons, or any other options provided by the plugin.

Save the Settings: After configuring the settings, make sure to save the changes.

Add Sharing Buttons to Your Website: The social sharing plugin will usually provide you with a couple of options to add the sharing buttons to your website. Here are two common methods:

a. Widget Area (when avaiabe): Many social sharing plugins offer a widget that you can add to your website's widget areas. Go to "Appearance" -> "Widgets" in your WordPress dashboard. Find the widget provided by the social sharing plugin, such as "Social Share Buttons" or "Social Icons," and drag it to the desired widget area, such as the sidebar or footer.

b. Shortcode or Template Tag: Some social sharing plugins provide a shortcode or template tag that you can insert directly into your website's pages or posts. Check the plugin documentation or settings page for instructions on using the shortcode or template tag. You can place it in your content editor wherever you want the sharing buttons to appear.

Preview and Test: View your website to see the social sharing buttons in action. Test the buttons by clicking on them to ensure they properly share your content to the selected social media platforms.

(25) WooCommerce

WooCommerce is a popular open-source e-commerce plugin for WordPress. It allows users to create and manage online stores, enabling them to sell products and services directly from their WordPress websites.

WooCommerce was created by three developers: Mark Forrester, Magnus Jepson, and Adii Pienaar. They initially developed a WordPress theme called "WooThemes" in 2008. Over time, they recognized the need for a robust e-commerce solution and launched WooCommerce as a plugin in September 2011.

In 2015, Automattic, the company behind WordPress.com, acquired WooThemes, including WooCommerce. This acquisition provided WooCommerce with significant resources, support, and integration possibilities within the WordPress ecosystem.

After its acquisition, WooCommerce experienced rapid growth and gained popularity among website owners looking to add e-commerce functionality to their WordPress sites.

WooCommerce's open-source nature, extensive customization options, and integration with various WordPress themes and plugins.

Importance of WooCommerce

WooCommerce empowers businesses to sell products and services online, expanding their reach and potential customer base. It offers flexibility, scalability, and a plethora of customization options to create a unique and branded online store experience. With its extensive plugin ecosystem, WooCommerce allows you to enhance your store's functionality as your business grows.

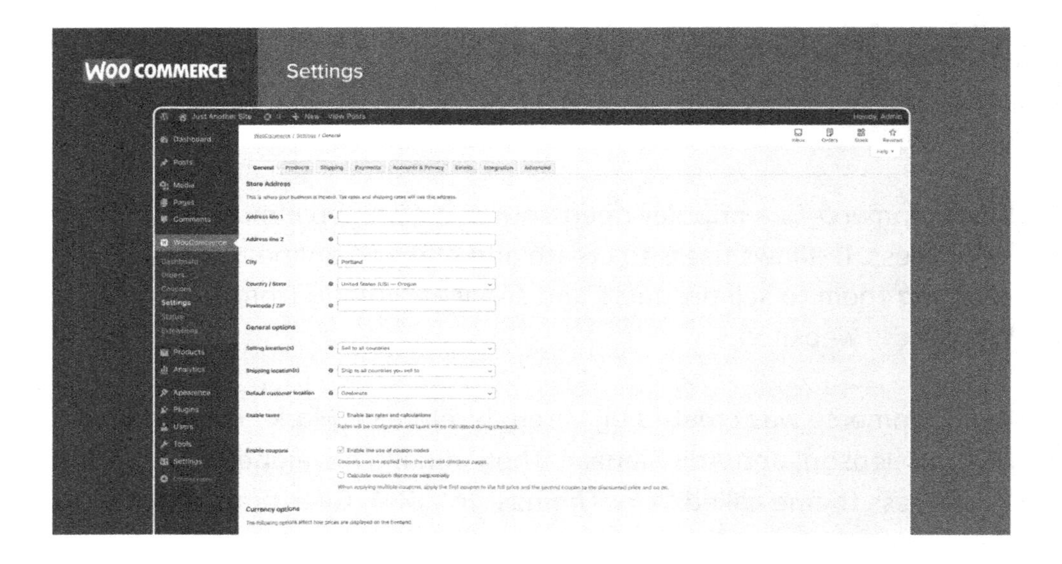

Installing WooCommerce

Installing WooCommerce is a straightforward process. Simply navigate to the "Plugins" section in your WordPress dashboard, click on "Add New," search for WooCommerce, and install and activate the plugin. WooCommerce will then guide you through a setup wizard to configure essential store settings.

Setting up WooCommerce

The setup wizard will help you configure fundamental aspects of your store, such as currency, shipping options, payment gateways, and tax settings. It also allows you to choose the pages for your store, including the shop page, cart page, and checkout page. You can customize these pages to align with your branding and design preferences.

Understanding the WooCommerce Panel

The WooCommerce panel in your WordPress dashboard provides a comprehensive overview of your store's performance, including sales, orders, inventory, and customer data. It also offers tools to manage coupons, discounts, and product reviews.

Payment Gateway

A payment gateway is a service that enables secure online transactions by facilitating the transfer of funds between the customer and the merchant. WooCommerce supports various payment gateways, including PayPal, Stripe, and Authorize.net, allowing you to offer multiple payment options to your customers.

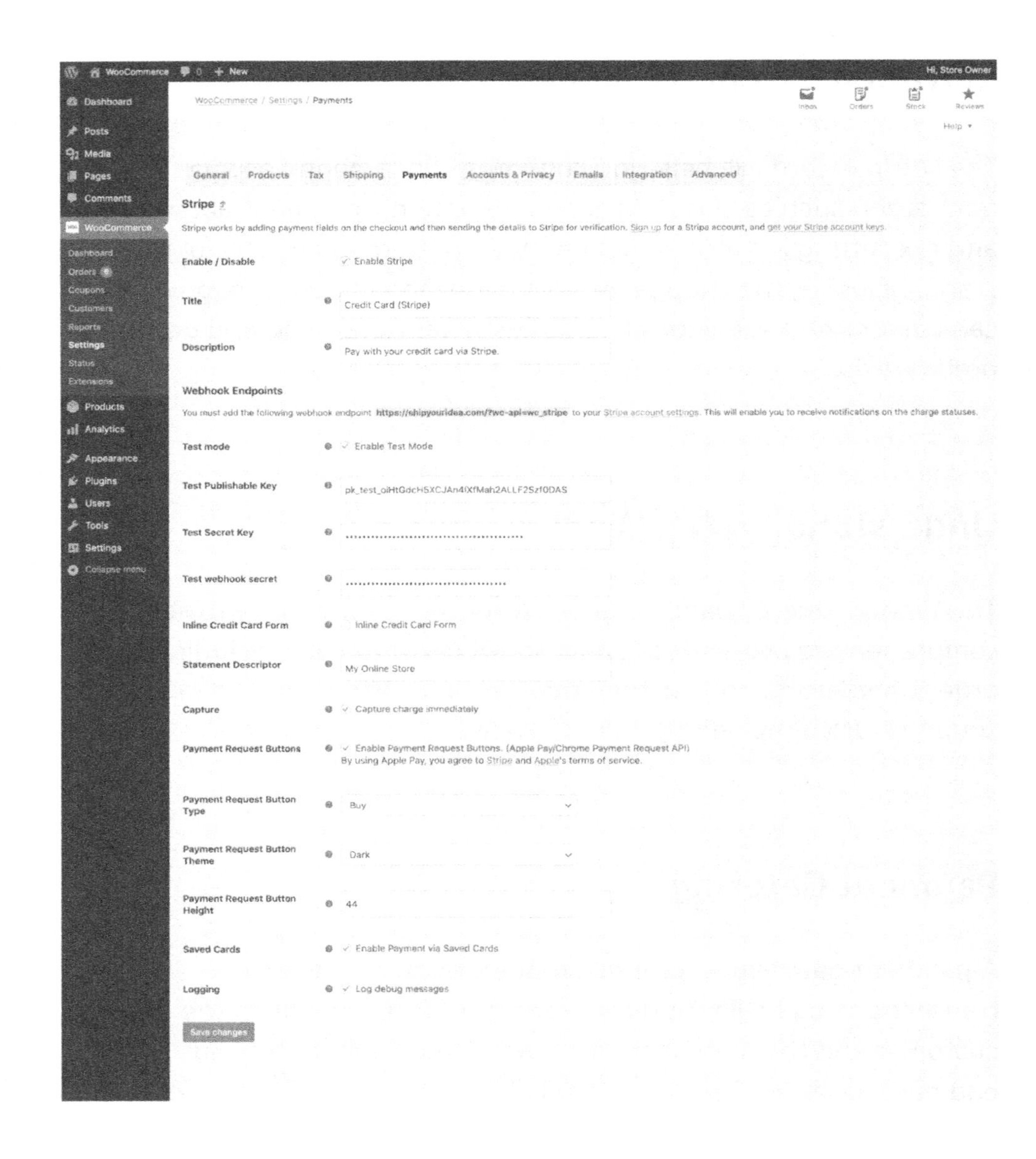

Products You Can Sell

With WooCommerce, you can sell physical products, digital downloads, memberships, subscriptions, and more. However, it is essential to comply with legal regulations and guidelines. Certain products, such as illegal items, drugs, firearms, and prohibited substances, cannot be sold using WooCommerce.

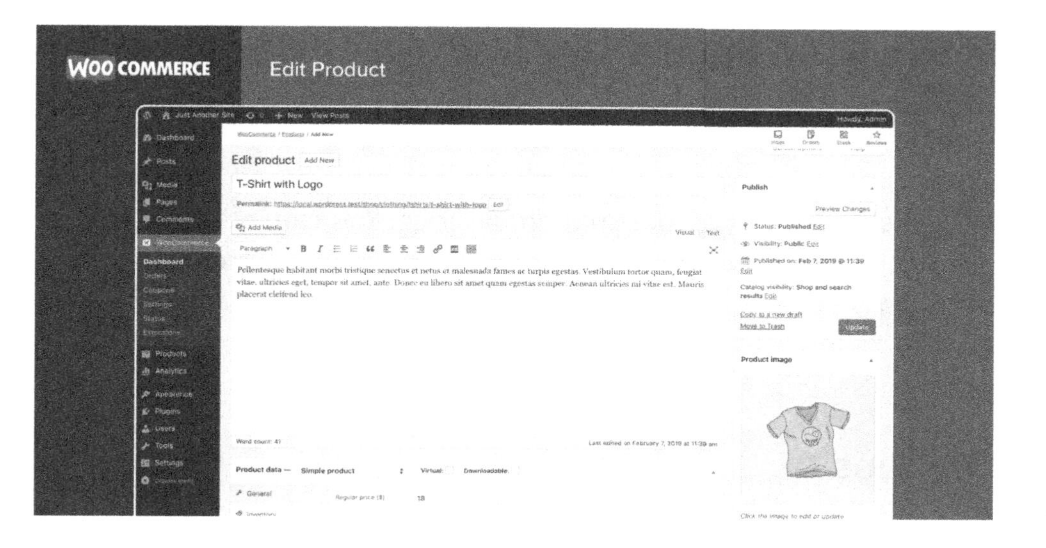

Product Types

WooCommerce offers various product types, such as simple products, variable products, grouped products, and external/affiliate products. Each product type caters to different scenarios and allows you to provide customers with various options, such as different sizes, colors, or configurations.

Adding Price, Specifications, and More

When adding products to your WooCommerce store, you can specify their price, inventory status, SKU, dimensions, weight, and other relevant specifications. You can also create product categories and tags to organize your inventory efficiently.

Shipping Products

WooCommerce provides built-in shipping functionality that allows you to set up shipping zones, methods, and rates based on various criteria such as weight, destination, or price. You can integrate with popular shipping carriers like UPS, FedEx, or USPS to streamline your shipping process.

Coupons

In WordPress, coupons refer to discount codes or vouchers that can be used by customers to avail discounts or special offers when making a purchase on a website.

Coupons serve as a promotional tool to attract customers, encourage sales, and reward loyal shoppers. They can be created and managed through the WooCommerce Coupons feature or with the help of additional coupon management plugins available in the WordPress ecosystem. With coupons, website owners can offer various types of discounts, such as a percentage off the total order, a fixed amount discount, free shipping, or buy-one-get-one (BOGO) deals. Coupons can have specific conditions and restrictions, such as minimum order value, limited usage per customer, validity dates, or restrictions to specific products, categories, or customer groups.

In the WordPress Admin Dashboard, go to "WooCommerce" and click on "Coupons." This will take you to the Coupons management page.

> **Add a New Coupon:** Click on the "Add Coupon" button to create a new coupon.
>
> **Configure the Coupon Details:** In the coupon creation page, you'll find various fields to configure the coupon. Some

important fields include:

Coupon code: Enter a unique code for the coupon. Customers will use this code to apply the discount during checkout.

Discount type: Choose the type of discount you want to offer, such as a percentage or fixed amount.

Coupon amount: Set the value of the discount.

Usage limit: Specify the number of times the coupon can be used.

Usage restriction: You can set conditions like minimum and maximum spend, limit usage to specific products or categories, restrict usage to specific customers, and more.

Expiry date: Set an expiration date for the coupon if desired.

Save the Coupon: After configuring the coupon details, click on the "Publish" or "Save" button to create and save the coupon.

Test the Coupon: It's always a good practice to test the coupon to ensure it works as intended. Add products to the cart on your WooCommerce store, proceed to the checkout page, and apply the coupon code to verify that the discount is correctly applied.

Understanding WooCommerce Sales

WooCommerce provides detailed sales reports, allowing you to analyze your store's performance, track revenue, and monitor product popularity. This information can help you make informed business decisions and optimize your marketing strategies.

Understanding WooCommerce Logs

WooCommerce logs provide a record of critical events and activities within your store, including errors, updates, and customer interactions. Logs can be helpful for troubleshooting issues and maintaining the security and stability of your store.

Problems with WooCommerce

While WooCommerce is a robust e-commerce solution, it may encounter occasional challenges. Common issues can include payment gateway configuration, inventory management, compatibility with themes or plugins, and performance optimization. Fortunately, there is a vast community and support available to assist you in resolving these problems.

WooCommerce is an invaluable tool for turning your WordPress website into a fully functional online store. By following the setup process and leveraging its extensive features, you can create a seamless and engaging shopping experience for your customers while managing your store efficiently.

(26) Malware

Malware in WordPress refers to any malicious software or code that is designed to infect and harm websites running on the WordPress content management system (CMS). WordPress is a popular platform for creating websites and blogs, and its widespread use makes it an attractive target for hackers and cybercriminals.

For Your Information

NEVER INSTALL NULLED THEMES.

Here are some common types of malware that can affect WordPress websites:

Backdoors: These are hidden entry points that allow attackers to gain unauthorized access to a website. Once they have access, hackers can manipulate files, steal data, or even take control of the site.

Spam Injectors: Malware can be used to inject spammy

content into a website, such as links to malicious websites, pharmaceutical advertisements, or other unwanted content. This can damage the site's reputation and impact its search engine rankings.

Phishing Pages: Malicious actors may create fake login or payment pages that mimic legitimate ones to steal user credentials or financial information.

Drive-by Downloads: Visitors to an infected WordPress site may unknowingly download malware onto their devices when they visit certain pages.

SEO Spam: Malware can be used to manipulate a site's SEO settings and rankings in search engine results, often by injecting keywords or links into the site's content.

Malicious Redirects: Attackers can set up redirects that take visitors to other malicious websites, potentially spreading malware or conducting further attacks.

Cryptojacking: Some malware infects websites to use their computing resources to mine cryptocurrency without the site owner's consent.

Ransomware: In some cases, malware can encrypt a website's files and demand a ransom for decryption.

Removing malware from a WordPress website can be a challenging task, but it's essential to ensure the security and integrity of your site. Here's a step-by-step guide on how to remove malware from WordPress:

Isolate the Infected Site: If you suspect malware on your WordPress site, take it offline or put it in maintenance mode to prevent further damage or spreading of malware to visitors.

Backup Your Website: Before making any changes, create a complete backup of your website, including files and databases. You can use WordPress backup plugins or your hosting control panel for this purpose.

Scan for Malware: Use a reputable security plugin to scan your website for malware. Some popular options include Wordfence, Sucuri Security, and MalCare. These plugins can identify infected files and provide guidance on how to clean them.

Identify and Remove Malicious Files: Once the security plugin identifies malicious files, follow its recommendations to remove or quarantine them. This often involves deleting or cleaning infected files.

Update WordPress Core, Themes, and Plugins: Ensure that your WordPress core, themes, and plugins are up to date. Outdated software is a common entry point for malware. Update everything to the latest versions.

Change Passwords: Change all passwords associated with your WordPress site, including the admin, FTP, and database passwords. Use strong, unique passwords to prevent further unauthorized access.

Remove Unnecessary Plugins and Themes: Delete any plugins or themes that you no longer use. Reducing your website's attack surface can help improve security.

Review and Repair the Database: Inspect your WordPress database for any suspicious or unauthorized entries. Clean up any potentially compromised data.

Check and Repair File Permissions: Ensure that file and directory permissions on your server are set correctly to prevent unauthorized access. Most files should be set to 644, and directories should be set to 755.

Monitor and Harden Security: Install a reputable security plugin and configure it to enhance your site's security. This may include setting up a firewall, enabling two-factor authentication, and implementing security headers.

Scan for Vulnerabilities: Regularly scan your site for vulnerabilities using security plugins or online tools. Address any vulnerabilities promptly.

Stay Informed: Keep yourself informed about the latest security threats and best practices in WordPress security to proactively protect your website.

Request Google Reconsideration (If Blacklisted): If your site was blacklisted by search engines due to malware, follow their guidelines to clean your site, and then request a reconsideration to remove the blacklist status.

Consider Professional Help: If you're unsure about removing malware or if the infection is severe, consider hiring a professional security expert or a WordPress developer who specializes in malware removal.

Removing malware often isn't a task for beginners because it involves knowledge of servers, source code, and cybersecurity.

(27)
Your Website

This book is the first step to you create a WordPress website. Remember, creating a website is an ongoing process. Continuously update and improve your content, and engage with your audience to maximize your website's impact.

With WordPress as your trusted platform, you have the power to create a professional and engaging website that represents your unique brand or message. So, what are you waiting for? Start your WordPress website-building journey today and unlock the endless possibilities that await you!

Now you can create a basic website with WordPress. If you check step-by-step this book, you can start right now your own website.

Check the book Build a WordPress WooCommence to start sell.

Let's remember

WordPress has earned its reputation as the go-to content management system (CMS) for website creation, and for good reason.

Here are just a few compelling reasons why you should consider using WordPress for your website:

Ease of Use: WordPress offers an intuitive and user-friendly interface, making it accessible even for beginners. You don't need to have extensive coding knowledge or technical expertise to get started.

Flexibility and Customization: With thousands of themes and plugins available, you can customize your website to suit your specific vision. From design elements to functionality enhancements, WordPress allows you to tailor your site to meet your unique requirements.

Content Management: WordPress excels at managing and organizing your content. Whether you're publishing blog posts, creating static pages, or adding media files, WordPress provides a streamlined workflow for content creation and organization.

SEO-Friendly: WordPress is designed with search engine optimization (SEO) in mind. Its structure and features make it easier for search engines to crawl and index your site, potentially boosting your visibility in search results.

Active Community and Support: WordPress boasts a vast community of users and developers who contribute to its continuous improvement. You'll find a wealth of resources, forums, and support channels to help you along your website-building journey.

Ready to get started? Remember to follow these simple steps to create your website using WordPress:

Choose a Domain and Hosting: Select a domain name that

reflects your brand or website purpose. Then, choose a reliable hosting provider that offers WordPress compatibility.

Install WordPress: Most hosting providers offer a one-click WordPress installation option. Follow the prompts and set up your WordPress site.

Select a Theme: Browse through the vast collection of WordPress themes, both free and premium, to find the one that aligns with your vision. Choose a theme that suits your website's purpose and appeals to your target audience.

Customize Your Site: Once you've installed a theme, you can customize it to match your brand identity. Add your logo, customize colors and fonts, and arrange your site's layout to create a visually appealing and cohesive design.

Add Content: Start adding content to your site, whether it's blog posts, pages, or media files. Utilize the WordPress editor, Gutenberg, to format and structure your content.

Enhance Functionality with Plugins: Extend the capabilities of your WordPress website by installing plugins. Plugins allow you to add features such as contact forms, social media integration, e-commerce functionality, and more.

Optimize for SEO: Take advantage of WordPress's SEO-friendly features and plugins to improve your website's search engine visibility. Optimize your content, meta tags, and URLs to enhance your chances of ranking higher in search results.

Preview and Publish: Before making your website live, preview your content and design to ensure everything looks and functions as intended. Once you're satisfied, hit that publish button and share your website with the world!

To have a good website, you need to invest in a good design and tools, like cache plugins. And your pages and posts contents can make the users like your website.

About the Author

Hi, I am Raphael Heide. I started the journey as a full stack and freelance designer in 2001. Working **remotely or in local** for agencies around the world, advising startups and collaborating with talented people to create digital products for commercial and consumer use.

I am a professional with a strong background in WordPress development, design, and cyber security. With a passion for technology and a keen interest in the web industry, I have dedicated my career to creating innovative solutions and ensuring the security of digital platforms.

Design

I believe that an aesthetically pleasing and user-friendly design plays a crucial role in the success of a website. By combining my technical expertise with a creative eye, I create visually appealing websites that effectively convey information, engage visitors, and reflect the brand identity of my clients.

Cyber Security

Given the increasing importance of online security, I have developed a strong focus on cyber security. I understand the potential threats and vulnerabilities that websites face and work diligently to implement robust security measures. From securing websites against malicious attacks to performing vulnerability assessments and providing recommendations for enhancing security, I prioritize safeguarding digital assets and ensuring data protection.

Online Support Material

To check the images present in these books and possible material updates, go to https://raphaelheide.com/books/wp2024

Build a WordPress Website From Scratch 2024

- Raphael Heide -